COMPELLING

ANDREEA IONELA BERINDEI

com·pel·ling

/kəmˈpeliNG/

adjective
evoking interest, attention, or admiration in a
powerfully irresistible way.

BERINDEI
ANDREEA IONELA

Copyright © 2021 ANDREEA IONELA BERINDEI.

All rights reserved. No part of this book may be used or reproduced by any means, graphic, electronic, or mechanical, including photocopying, recording, taping or by any information storage retrieval system without the written permission of the author except in the case of brief quotations embodied in critical articles and reviews.

WestBow Press books may be ordered through booksellers or by contacting:

WestBow Press
A Division of Thomas Nelson & Zondervan
1663 Liberty Drive
Bloomington, IN 47403
www.westbowpress.com
844-714-3454

Because of the dynamic nature of the Internet, any web addresses or links contained in this book may have changed since publication and may no longer be valid. The views expressed in this work are solely those of the author and do not necessarily reflect the views of the publisher, and the publisher hereby disclaims any responsibility for them.

Any people depicted in stock imagery provided by Getty Images are models, and such images are being used for illustrative purposes only.
Certain stock imagery © Getty Images.

Scripture quotations marked (NLT) are taken from the Holy Bible, New Living Translation, copyright ©1996, 2004, 2015 by Tyndale House Foundation. Used by permission of Tyndale House Publishers, a Division of Tyndale House Ministries, Carol Stream, Illinois 60188. All rights reserved.

Scripture quotations marked HCSB are taken from the Holman Christian Standard Bible®, Copyright © 1999, 2000, 2002, 2003, 2009 by Holman Bible Publishers. Used by permission. Holman Christian Standard Bible®, Holman CSB®, and HCSB® are federally registered trademarks of Holman Bible Publishers.

ISBN: 978-1-6642-3909-8 (sc)
ISBN: 978-1-6642-3911-1 (hc)
ISBN: 978-1-6642-3910-4 (e)

Library of Congress Control Number: 2021913309

Print information available on the last page.

WestBow Press rev. date: 8/4/2021

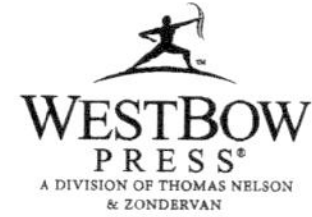

Acknowledgments

To the **One** who literally makes my heart beat. I love **You**. I owe it all to **You**.

Contents

Introduction

When I was young, I had a hard time expressing my feelings, thoughts, and opinions. Writing made everything easier, so I journaled in privacy. As an adult, I still do. Writing this book almost feels like I'm putting my journal into your hands. But it will be more than that because my paintings express my heart, and these words expose my thoughts.

As you go through these pages, I ask that you linger on each one. As you do so, please know these have been painted in tender moments with extraordinary amounts of grace, sacrifice, and dedication. While I hope you find yourself through these pages, more so, I hope you will read and look through this book with an open heart.

As I write this, I remember a time when I wanted to change the world. I have always believed there is a role for me to fulfill that only I can because of how I was created. I think that stands true for all of us. We all have gifts lying underneath, waiting to be discovered and developed. But until we take time to ask ourselves why we were put on this earth, these gifts are dormant. It's up to us.

Naturally, I'm an inquisitive person. I like to create, discover, learn, and grow. I want answers, and I seek them. Maybe that's how this book came to be...

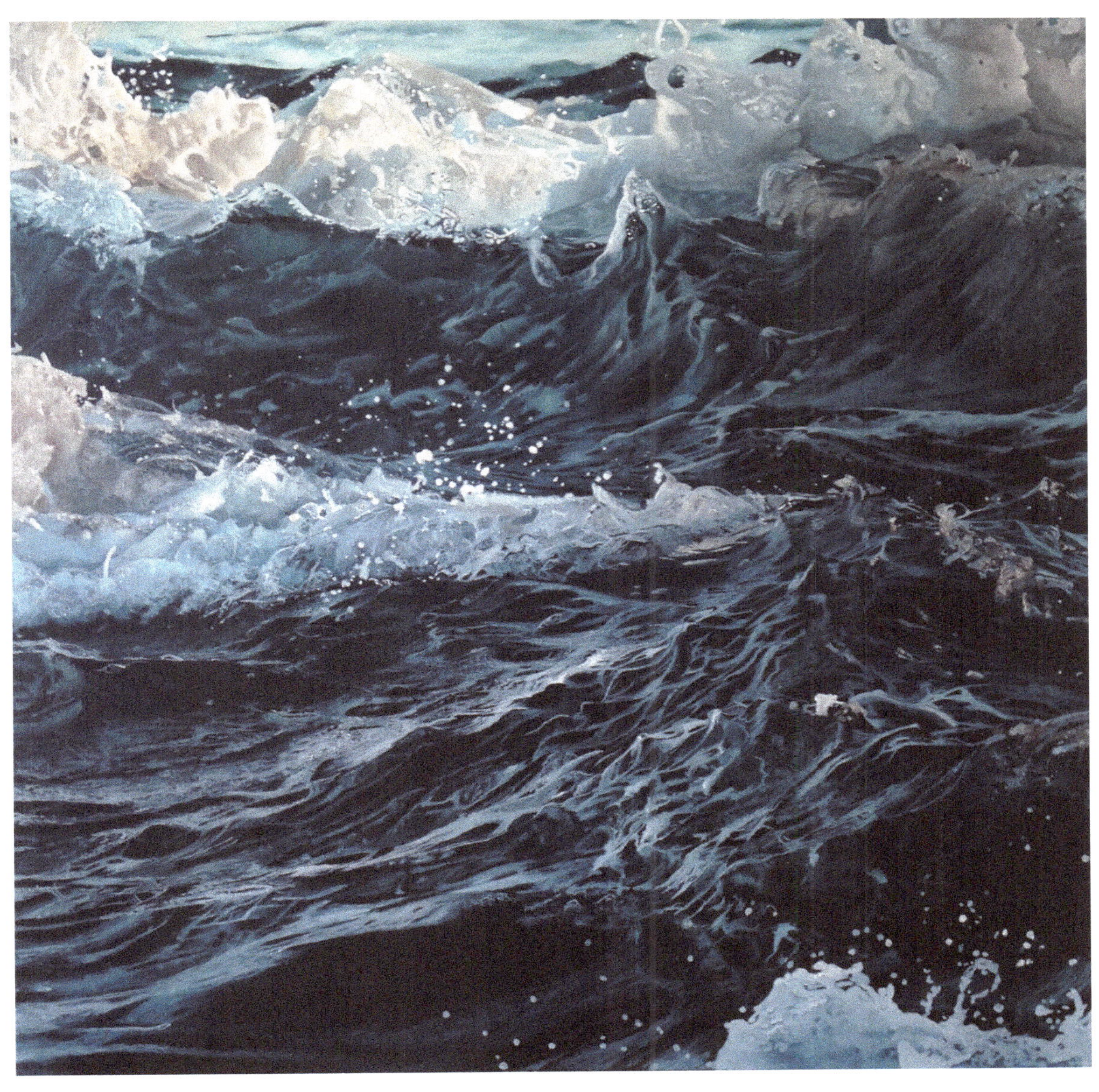

"A Promise"

Her deep-set brown eyes glanced out the open window, fixating on the first light of morning. The central-eastern skies were slightly smeared with clouds. As the rays of sunshine found their way through, the small valley came to life. Rivers met and crossed paths, surrounded by lofty, majestic mountains on the heights of which eagles raced with the wind.

She loved the wind. The breeze that now caressed her short brown hair always seemed to whisper her name. *Valiant Warrior*, that's what her name meant. You could describe her beauty, not in her finely traced eyebrows or long eyelashes but in her peaceful presence and lively movements.

The children played outside, swinging and chasing after each other. She longed to play with them; she could overhear them giggling together. She bit her bottom lip to stop herself from laughing out loud. She wanted to go outside, but the delight was short-lived. Her tall slim frame slumped as she tiptoed from the window back to her homework. She never liked school and was convinced that she wasn't the smartest. Wasn't that what her teachers said under their breath?

She had passion in her small heart, a desire that was growing. She wanted to change the world but knew she could not do it on her own. The girl was often told she was timid, difficult, and aloof. Deep down, she longed to belong and be appreciated.

Instead, she often felt like a stranger in this big world. A world she was not sure what role she had to play. While the girl felt alone, she was comforted by choosing to do the right thing. Later on, she would find she had strengths she was unaware of. Her purpose would put her in circumstances and around people that will highlight both her strengths and weaknesses.

She was a young woman now, trying to open doors of the past and sort through memories. It was so easy for her to remember those who ignored her; they caused so much pain. But there were others who deserved true attention—the ones who made her feel at home and wanted to be part of her life. The teacher, the preacher, the neighbor, the coach, the leader, the friend, the sisters, and the parents made her feel seen. When she thought of these people, she forgot the pain and was filled with gratitude.

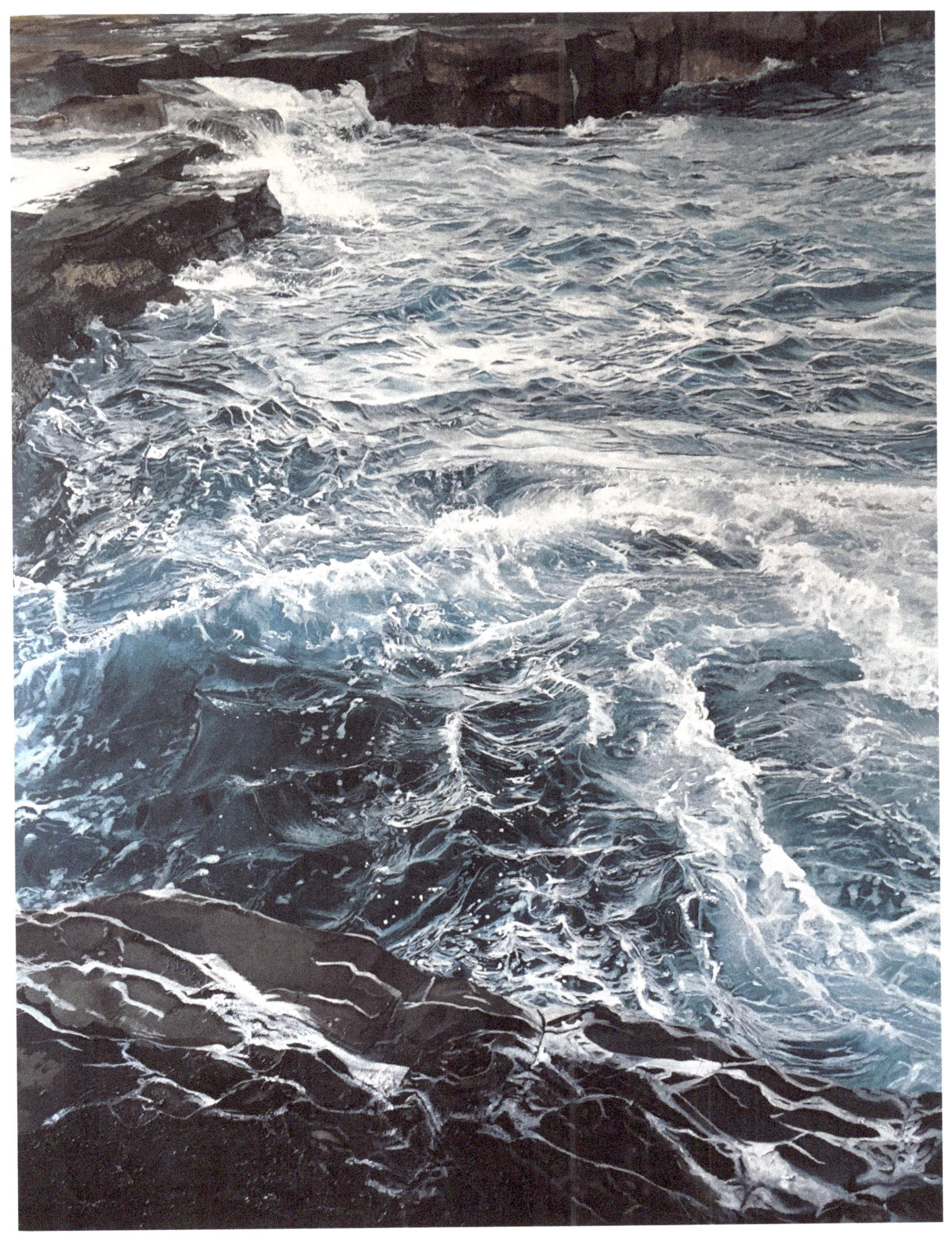

"Not Too Long Ago"

When you choose to discover your gifts, you are in a unique place. You are on your way to finding out what you were born to do, the thing you are or will be passionate about doing. When you have passion, you don't consider what you love to do as an option but necessary. You deny yourself instant gratification because you are willing to sacrifice for what you believe to be true about your gift. If you see potential, you will invest in it and envision the future return of it.

Not all fingers are equal, and neither are gifts. A gift is free, but it's not cheap; it will be inconvenient at times. People carry their future on their shoulders by the purchases they make. You have to have to be intentional with your time and resources. Immediate pleasures have to be sacrificed for the gift and personal growth. The quantity of life in fun and friendships must be substituted for quality of life with family and the task at hand. The friends that I choose to keep around me, the music I listen to, and the movies I watch can either add to my life or subtract it daily. It's a choice. No matter how gifted you are, it will not develop itself if you don't invest in yourself and your gift.

I don't believe in luck. I believe in dedication, sacrifice, and discipline. If I see you succeeding at something in life, I know these choices were made. Nothing just happens. I am responsible for myself when I make a choice. When the choice is made for me, someone else will be accountable for my lack of productivity and the consequences that follow. I was born free with a choice in my lifestyle.

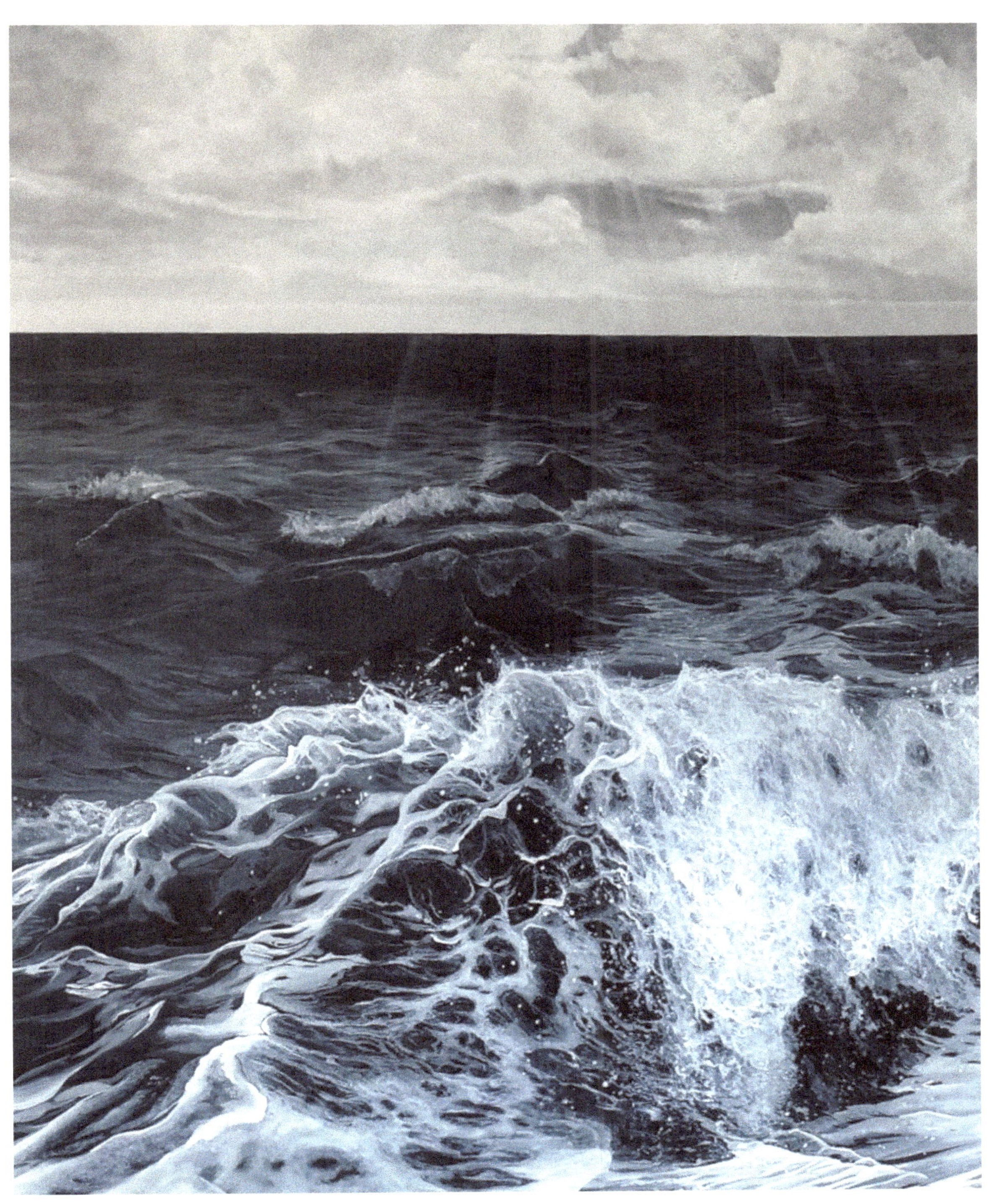

"Compelling"

Wisdom, compassion, kindness, and gentleness should be what we should strive for. Reflect each day on the areas where you want growth.

We are found lacking in the issues that have eternal value. Acknowledging our shortcomings should challenge us to grow. If I was to ask you about your achievement, I'm sure you could indulge me for a few hours. If I was to ask about your failures, it could take weeks or months. We avoid talking about our shortcomings because we don't want the people we love or those we mentor to see we can be wrong. We hide behind nice cars, clothes, status, and other possessions.

Do you want to be known as the woman who had excellent fashion taste? Do you want to be known as the man who treated his car nicer than his sister, mother, or wife? We mishandle the true blessings because we don't know their actual worth. Anyone can change the way they dress or improve their skill. The inside process, however—the mental attitude, humility, generosity, hospitality, and honor—does not come cheap. We would rather quit than keep trying. Compassion, love, joy, and peace are what everyone craves. It takes humility and maturity to become aware of how little patience we have with others and ourselves. A person who dresses nicely but has a controversial character makes you run the opposite direction, but rarely will you see someone slapping you for being kind.

What is the worth of time? Be around someone who is dying. What is the value of sleep? Be around someone who lacks it. What is the cost of health? Hear the cries of those with chronic pain. What is the value of relationships? Have a conversation with a lonely person. What is the worth of eyesight? Spend time with someone who cannot see. Reflecting on life, taking responsibility for how we spend it, and deciding who should be part of it are the wisest places to start.

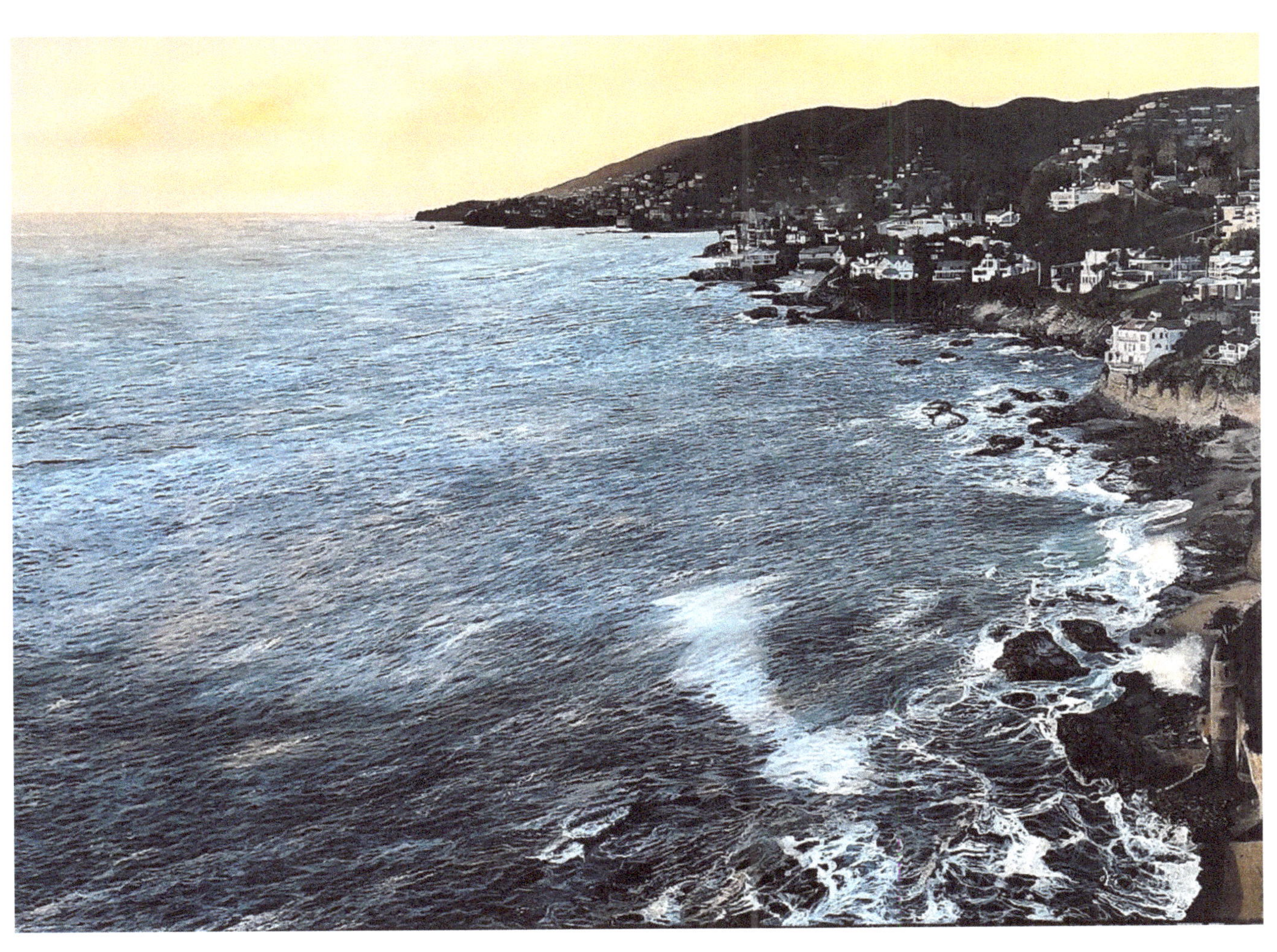

"Time Is The Coin Of Your Life"

Joy and Happiness were two sisters. Many thought they were twins because they looked so much alike, but compared closely, things were not as they seemed. Sure enough, after spending time with them, one would notice a striking difference.

Happiness showed up on more occasions; that's why everyone seemed to like her. She was well-liked, pleasant, youthful, and careless. She was there to share a good laugh, put a smile on someone's face, or hug those who accomplished success. She always seemed to be there, first to come and last to leave.

But Joy was different. From how she carried herself to how she looked at people with confidence, Joy came to stay. She was found with the trustworthy, persevering, and disciplined. Joy was not known to be fair-weathered. She was there even when everything became quiet after the others went home; you could count on this sister to hang around. She was reliable, truthful, and carried strong morals.

Contrary to her younger sister, Joy made sure she was around the right company and in the right situations. She would not be found in the house of gossip, lust, pride, or selfishness. To those who had never been around her, she was a stranger. To those who had known her and lost her presence, she was terribly missed. People without her in their lives were miserable.

Anyone who became her friend would not exchange her for all the pleasures in the world. Joy could not be manipulated, controlled, or abused. The Prince of Peace was her Sovereign. She was best friends with Wisdom. Humility was her teacher; Righteousness, her shield and bodyguard. Faith and Hope were her neighbors, and she hung around the triplets named Goodness, Gentleness, and Generosity. The narrow path that led to life was where she could be found, keeping company with the faithful. Joy could never be chastised, for she knew her timing well. She was never late nor early. This was all because of her complete devotion and submission to her Maker, the Greatest Force, Love.

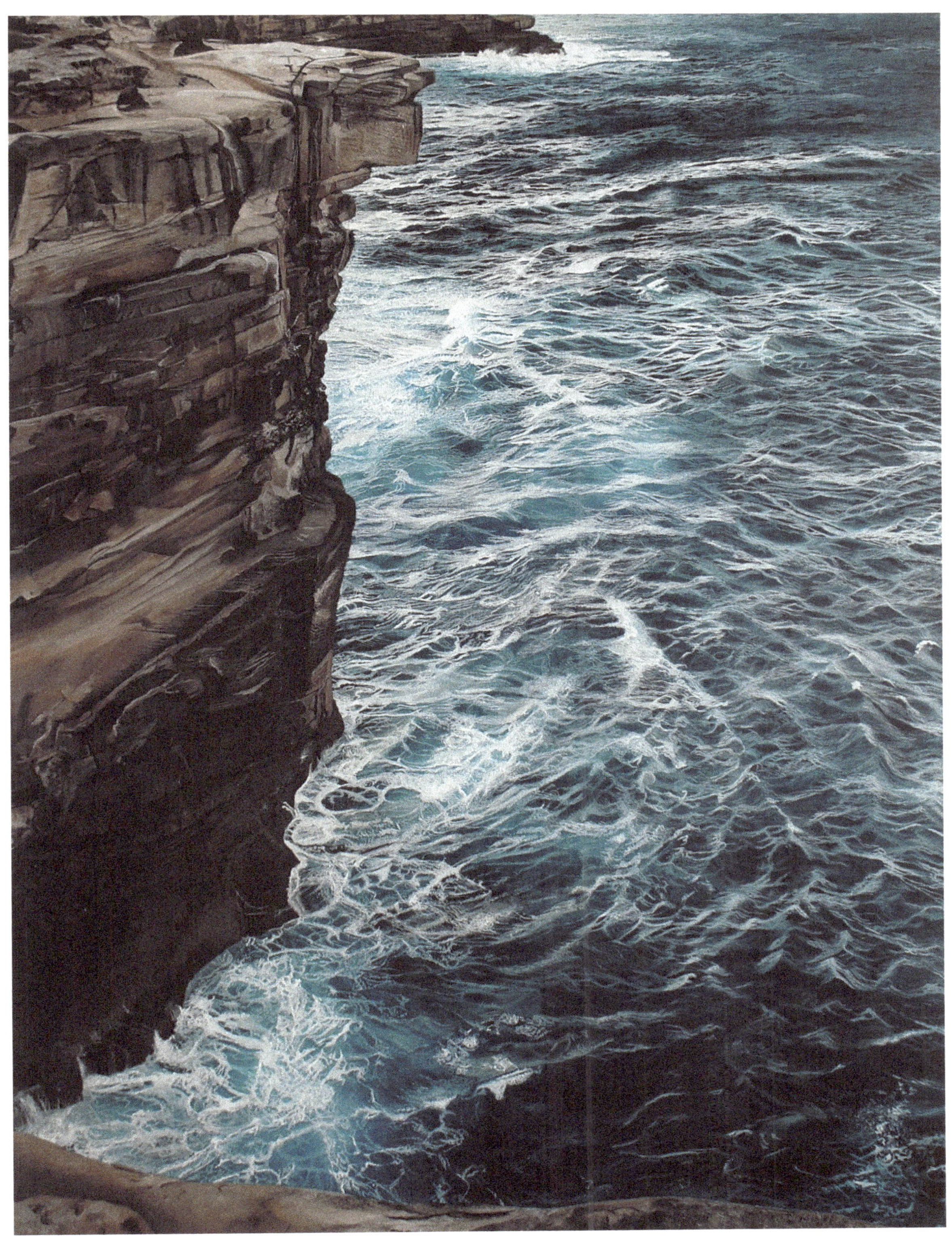

"About This Time"

I've read and heard of rare people who trained under harsh circumstances to win races and marathons. examples of this are those from a Third World country with a dream to compete in the Olympics. They didn't have the right equipment to train with and usually would have to work harder than others. They didn't have paved roads to run on—they had only rugged roads, steep climbs, and down slopes. Their body knew how to handle hard conditions. Most of the people I know or read about that have accomplished something inspiring were less privileged; they built stamina under challenging circumstances. The training was not pleasant. It required discipline to fight past shortcomings.

My training started with after-school chores and obeying rules even when I thought I knew better. When walking to school, it did not matter whether it rained or snowed; I still had to walk to get there. I attended school whether I felt like it or not because I knew a diploma was at the end of the journey. When I first started painting, I worked with cheap materials, hoping to grow my skill. I would be found painting in good, bad, natural, and artificial light, as I would try to learn. These were the moments of training that refined me into who I am today.

I believe that what we overcome will launch us into our next season and bring breakthroughs. Just like passing a test, we move forward into the next grade. But unless we learn the value of each lesson, we may repeat it until we do.

My passion for painting comes from my calling. It is my purpose, which comes from God alone. But you have to make a personal decision to pursue the gift. Once you do, you will discover that you do have what it takes to achieve your destiny.

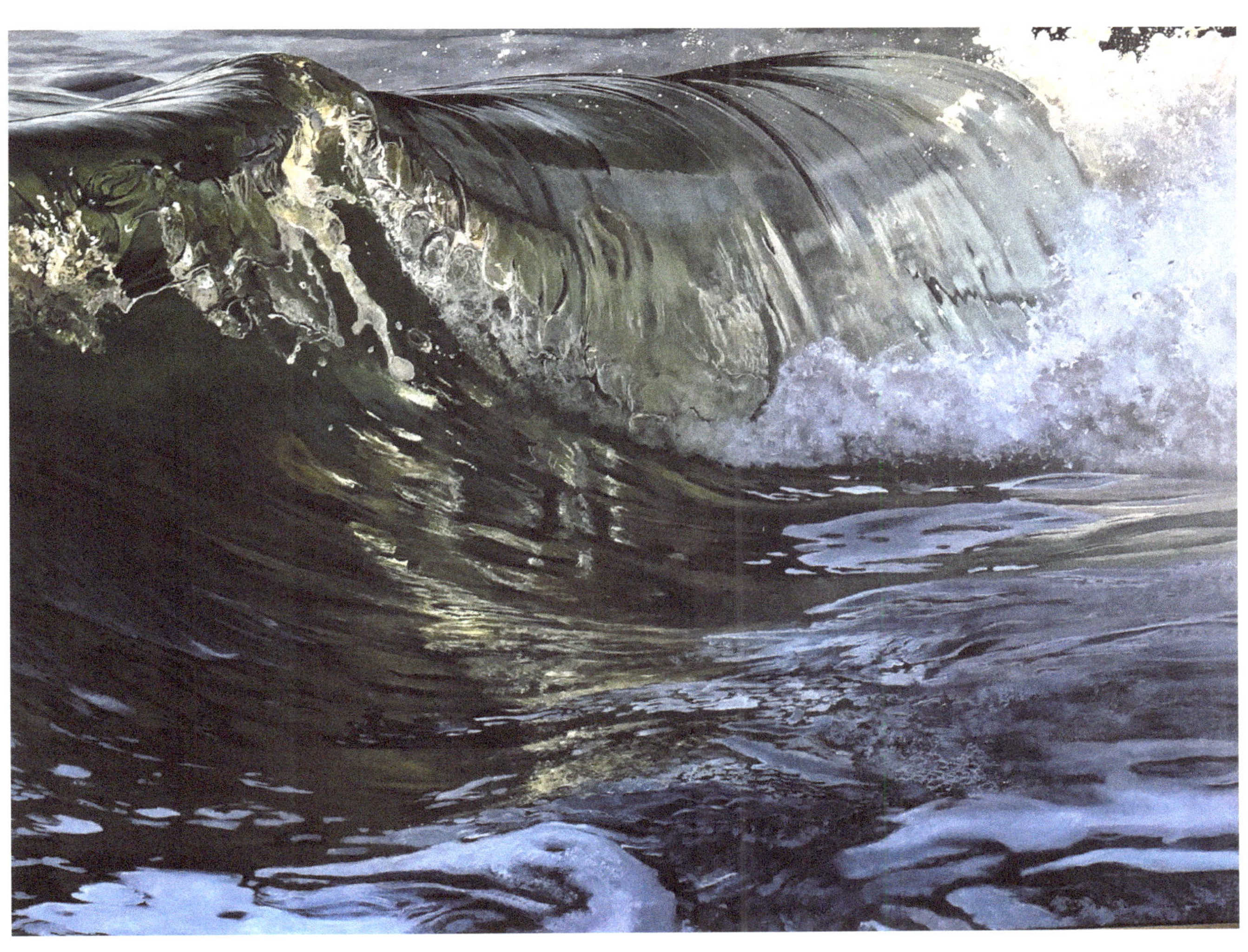

"Endurance"

"The Lord made me at the beginning of His creation, before His works of long ago. I was formed before ancient times, from the beginning, before the earth began. I was born when there were no watery depths and no springs filled with water. I was delivered before the mountains and hills were established, before He made the land, the fields, or the first soil on earth. I was there when He established the heavens, when He laid out the horizon on the surface of the ocean, when He placed the skies above, when the fountains of the ocean gushed out, when He set a limit for the sea so that the waters would not violate His command, when He laid out the foundations of the earth. I was a skilled craftsman beside Him. I was His delight every day, always rejoicing before Him."

- Proverbs 8:22-30 [HCSB]

Who was she really? Where could you find her?

If you asked the birds of the air or the wild animals, they were oblivious. She cannot be found among the earth's riches. Men look for her through ancient tunnels inscribed by mortals who prided themselves that they had guidance to her. Discovering the origins of rivers, they thought they came near, but the stratosphere couldn't contain her. She is the mother of virtues.

Her name was Wisdom, last name Insight. Her depth and height and her length and width have no set measures. She savors and relishes truth but cannot stand the taste of evil. Her words are not twisted or skewed. Among her are those of disciplined lives. You cannot squander your precious life if you obey her, for anyone who listens is alert and responsive. A lucrative career cannot be compared with what she has to offer. The desires of this word cannot hold a candle to her. With the help of her legitimate authority, lawmakers legislate fairly and governors govern. Wisdom's appearances are so rare, many have only heard rumors of them.

Sanity, Knowledge, and Discretion live in her neighborhood; they know each other well. Her daily companions are Glory and Honor. Righteousness and Justice live down the street. She hates Evil with a passion, as well as his younger daughters, Pride and Arrogance. Common sense and counsel could not be found on their lips.

You would think everyone would embrace her; however, many are filled with hate, which damages their soul. They flirt with death as they wrong and reject her.

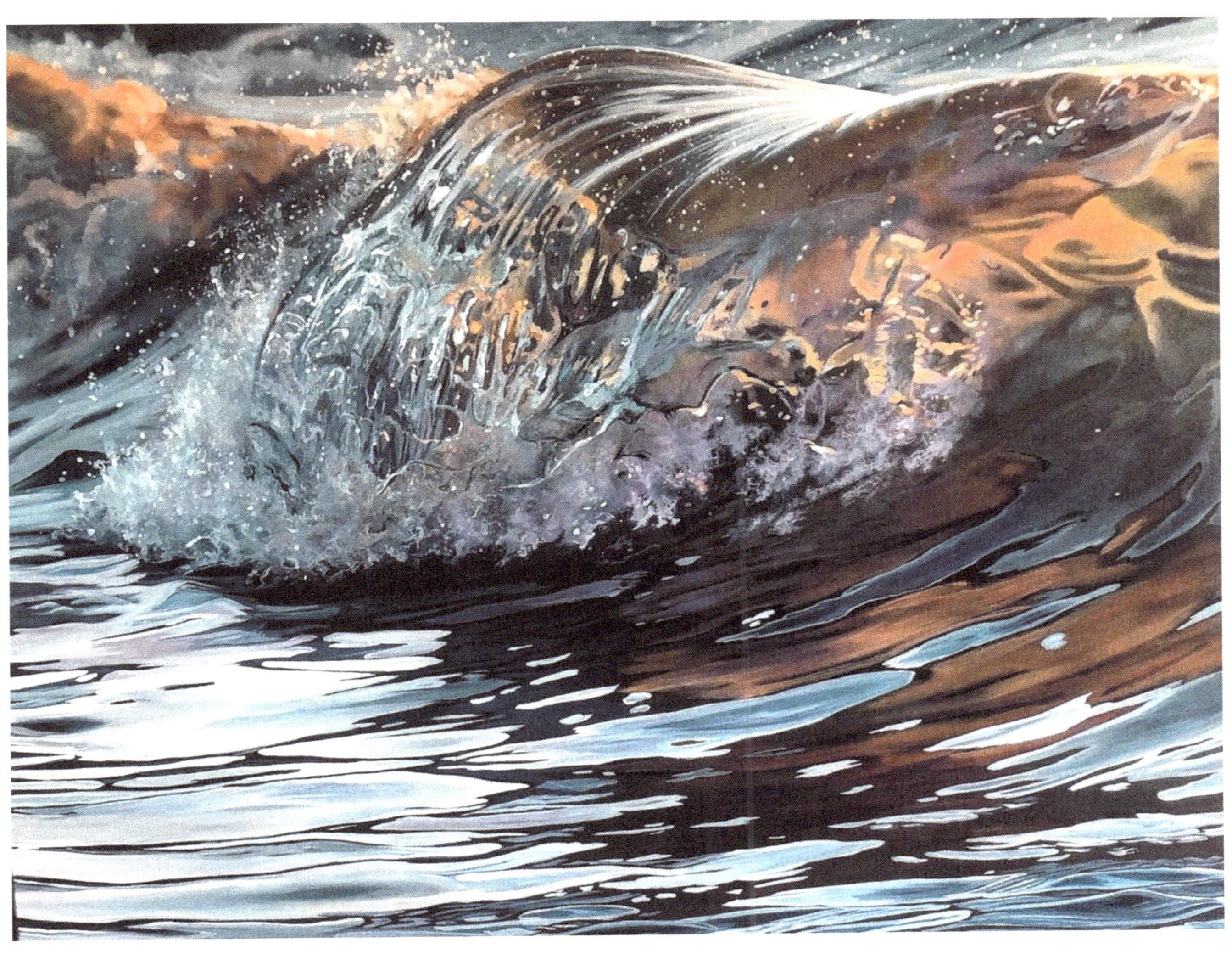

"The Journey Of One Thousand Miles"

People are surprised at the fruit their lives bring forth. Reaping what you sow tends to have a bad connotation.

Many planted faithfully, paying the price of early mornings and late nights. They gave more than was required. Some are praised for skills they have, inventions developed, or how children are raised. We call these people faithful. They gave when no one was watched; they went the extra mile. They were consistent, even if they were called foolish.

You are called be faithful and stay wherever you are planted right now. Don't deviate off-course because you see others become successful seemingly overnight. You see others ahead although they started after you; however, you have the better results. You may look foolish, but keep going. You may feel uncertain, but continue moving forward.

I have been given bad advice in the past. I don't believe those who gave it wanted me to fail—they couldn't feel what I felt or understand the passion behind the gift. Although it came in the form of a seed, the promise came. I believed, treasured, and, instead of hiding, chose to water it with my tears and the sweat of my brow. I watered the seed when it was too small to be seen, when I looked for encouragement, or I needed a hand to pull me up when I was down. I had to push through when my work was mocked and ridiculed. I had to keep watering, despite thoughts of defeat and weeds of doubt trying to take over the roots.

When I didn't believe in myself anymore, there was One who stayed closer than a brother. He believed in me. He was my cheerleader, comforter, and Only hope. He is the reason I do what I do.

If you appreciate someone's work, ask them their motivation; what they did it for when no one watched. It's easy to do something when everyone believes in you. What if you had to do it on your own, with no one to encourage? Would you find excuses? You reap what you sow. You can't expect to reap good if you plant evil or reap evil if you have been faithful by planting good.

"A good person produces good things from the treasury of a good heart, and an evil person produces evil things from the treasury of an evil heart."
- Matthew 12:35 [NLT]

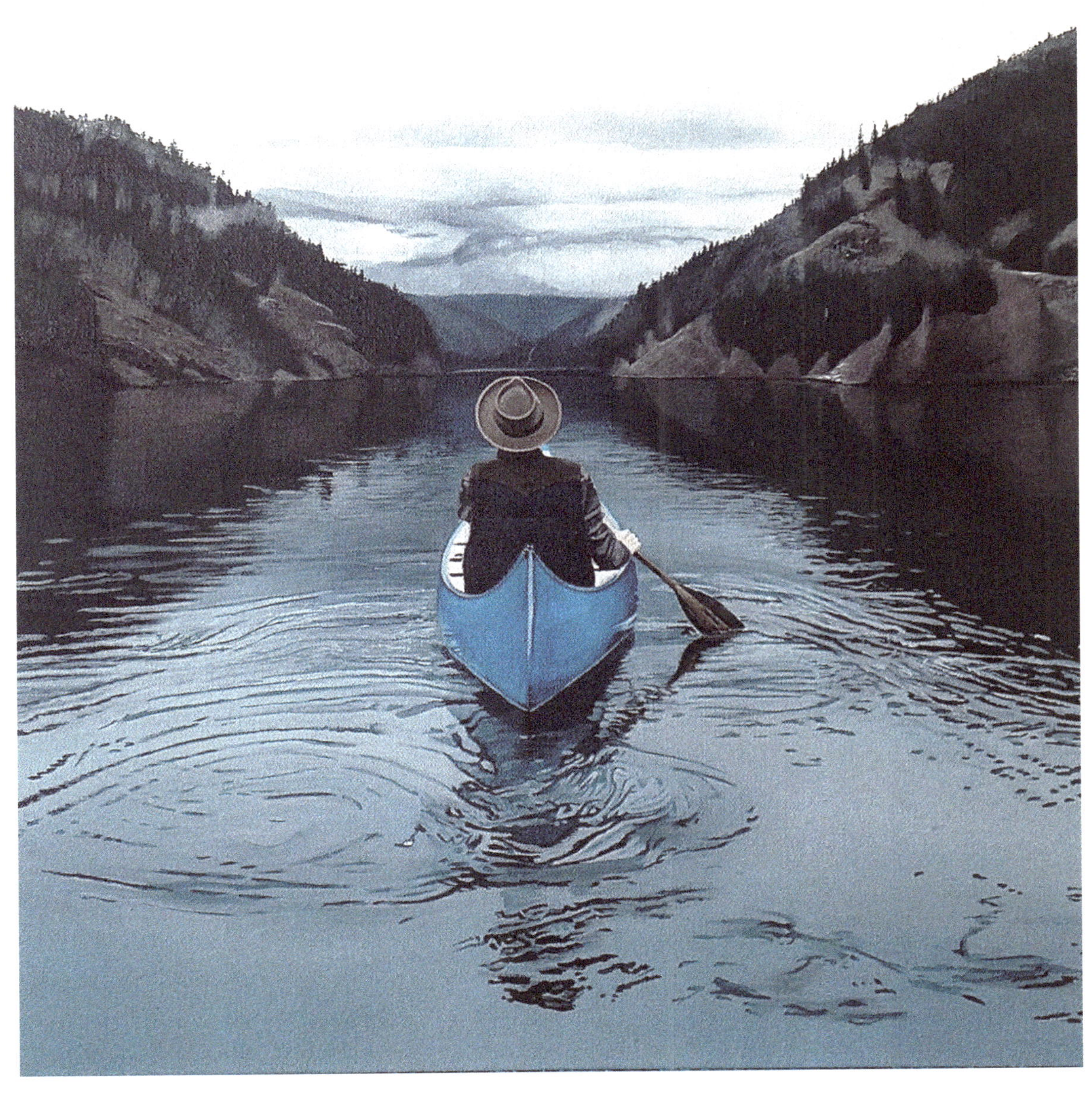

"A Reason To Hope"

Watching the sunset, she noticed how those around her tried to capture the beauty through the cameras they held. By now, she knew better. She knew by trying to capture the best moments, she would end up missing them. She could surely talk about the beauty of a sunset captured, but she could not speak about the way it made her feel. To acknowledge the fullness of a moment, she had to be present.

So, there she was, watching. She pulled the collar of her jacket closer; it was getting colder as the sun slowly sunk beyond the horizon. Lovers around her held hands, grandparents cuddled together, and children took advantage of the little light they had left. Her eyes drifted towards the distance. There was a beautiful boat sailing calmly. She wondered if those on the boat had a more pleasant view of the sunset.

She paused, realizing that the work of art being painted before her eyes by the invisible hand of the Creator was more striking because the boat was in it. She was sure that those on it could not know that the sunset was more picturesque for her. Her thoughts trailed away, lost in the beauty before her...

How many times do we want to be the main subject in life? We want the boat or, at least, to be on it. We crave attention but hardly, if ever, experience it ourselves. I think we all wonder how it would feel sometimes. For someone else, our lives look beautiful from the outside. They might think we have it all together, no ups, downs, or delays. Some only see the sunset and how beautiful the boat sails, but those on the boat have experienced the storms. Not every day looks or feels like a beautiful sunset. Everyone we admire has put in the extra effort. There is no fast-forward button on their lives, but we would choose the fast-track and complain later about the results if given the opportunity.

There is a truth that we don't like to hear. When we go through pain, we want an easy exit. However, the birth of anything requires process, patience, and pain. To have something you have never had, you have to do something you have never done. May we learn not to rush the process of greatness. Not every day is a storm, nor every day a sunset. If you don't quit, you will catch a break.

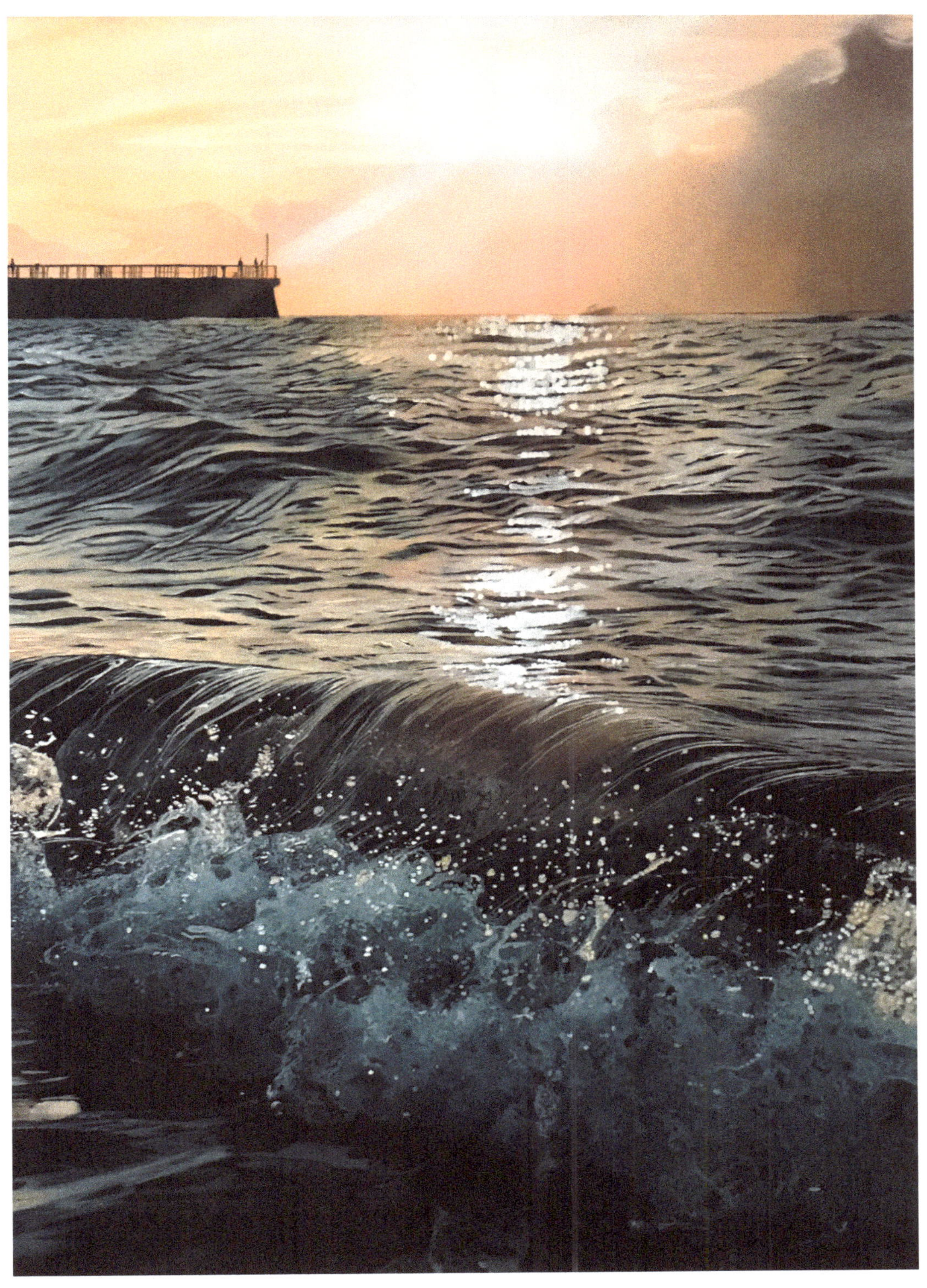

"Sunsets And Storms"

"The way to love anything is to realize that it might be lost."
- G. K. Chesterton

The bitter will not last, nor the sweetness of tender moments. This is why we want more from life. Sometimes, the journey to another glorious moment can be long and arduous, leaving us discontent. A day turns into a week, a week into a month, a month into a year, and a year into a decade.

I am there right now. I understand the waiting process. I know the journey of surrendered expectations, renewed passion, and regained hope. However, no matter how bad we have it, there will always be someone who has it worse or better. Pain and joy are universal.

Some people are praying for what you take for granted. Too much bliss will turn us into feathers; too much hardship can turn us into barbed wire. Before you complain or give into ungratefulness, reflect upon the blessings you do have. While you buy a new pair of shoes, someone doesn't have feet. While you complain about a car, someone only wishes to drive themselves around again. Even as I write this, someone's eyes have seen their last sunset. Oh, the things we take for granted. The fact that we get to live another mundane day is both a blessing and a miracle.

I have friends who fascinate me. Although they are burdened by sorrow and trials, they are as light as the sound of a bell. They have reasons to be dejected, yet they are patient and generous. They bear kind smiles and warm hugs, no matter how hard of a day they have faced. They are not held back in self-pity. Instead, their mindset reflects a belief that the best is yet to come. I am constantly challenged to have a positive outlook on life. If they can have it, so can I.

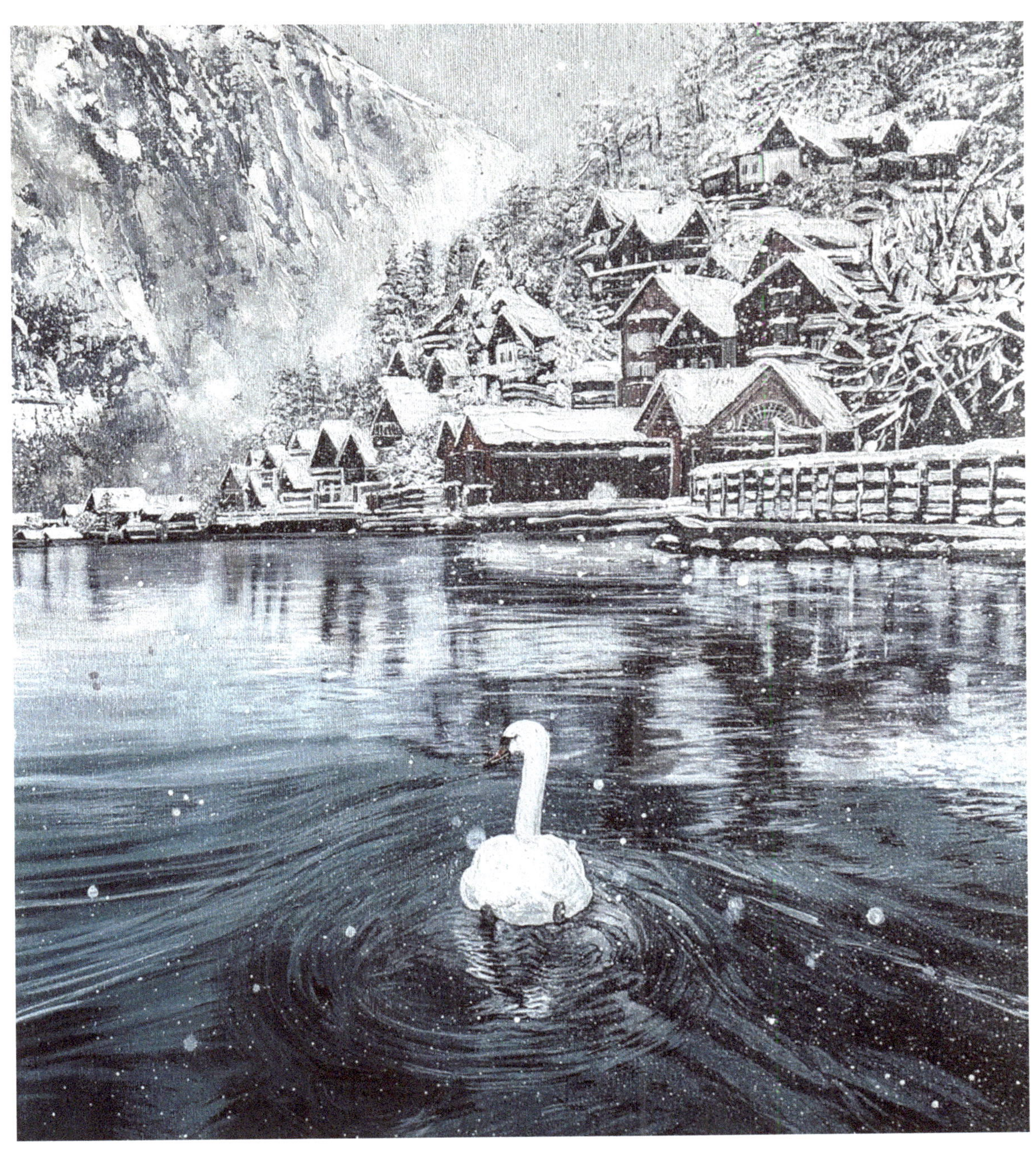

"Wait And Hope"

The chilly air sent a shiver through her body as she put her hands in her pockets. Inhaling deeply, she closed her eyes, stopping for a moment to take it all in.

As daylight spread to the ends of the earth, dawn rose from the east and commanded the morning to appear. What a scene that was painted before her eyes. The water seemed so free. Or was it really? The waves, while unrestrained, burst out of earth's womb, still had its boundaries—the shore was its limit. What is freedom, to run away from troubles and experience no pain? To be free of cares?

We are slaves to whatever controls us. Anger can make you have outbursts of frustration. Selfishness can make you look out for your interests. Superficiality can make one look for a good time. Stinginess can make you do as little as you can for others. Hopelessness can make you crush your hope and of those around you. Our opinion of others is a reflection of our opinion of ourselves.

True freedom means to be free of the opinion of others. We are quick to forgive criticism, selflessly give to those in need, and not assume the worst of others. Those who are free are generous, kind, gentle, and forgiving. To her, freedom meant to conquer evil with good.

"Do not be conquered by evil, but conquer evil with good."
- Romans 12:21[HCSB]

Everything pure, lovely, and worthy of admiration in her was from the One who instilled these virtues within her. The One she always felt nearby. The One she more or less aware of in the days, weeks, years that followed. She was unique and gifted—she was His investment. Many things she thought would disqualify her became the areas that qualified her. The Greatest Influence she has came through the scars of her own life when they were redeemed. She would live only for the applause of His nail-scarred hands.

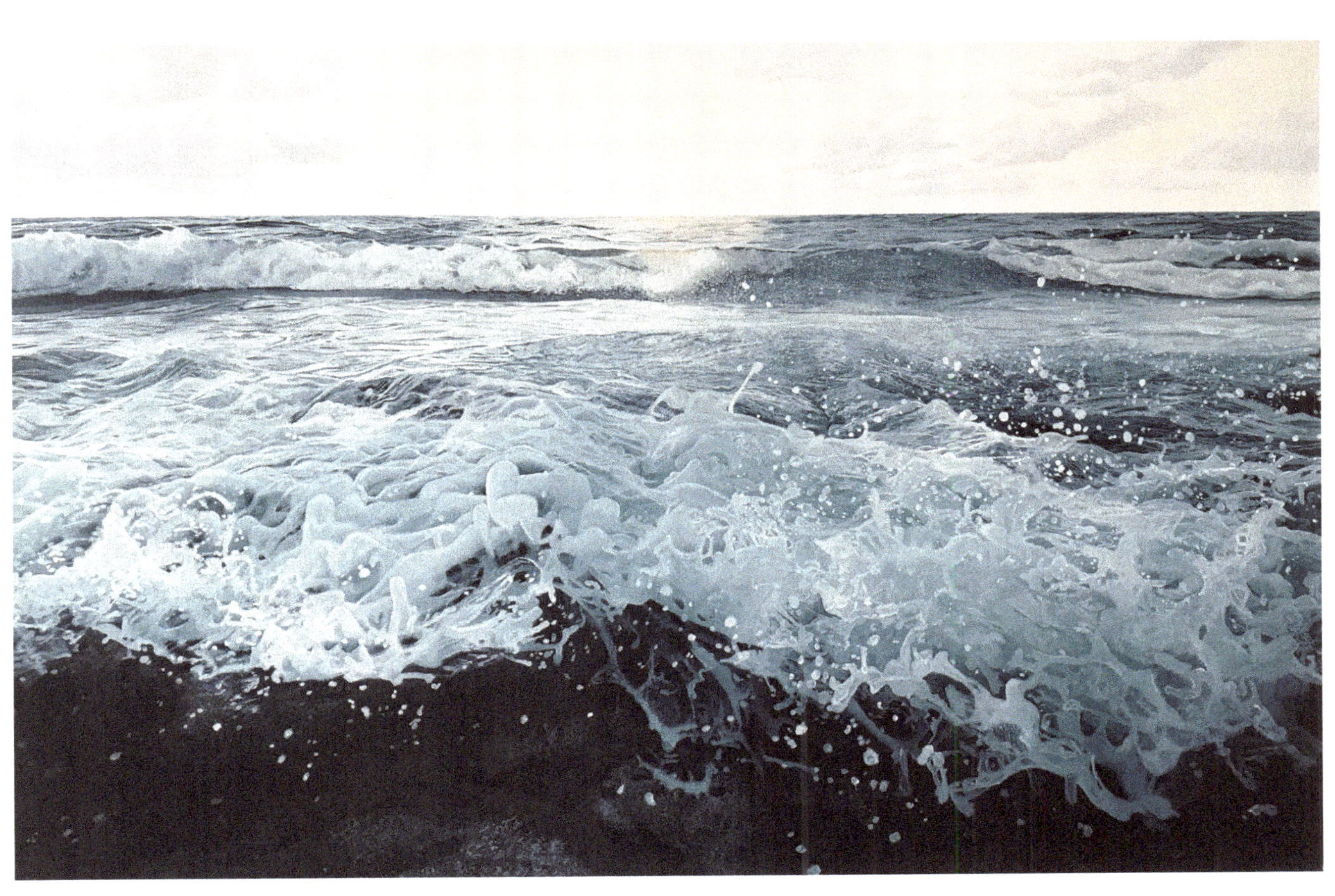

"Pure Heart"

It was one of those days where she was face-to-face with her future. She struggled to look straight ahead. She wanted to accomplish greatness, but the fear of what people would say and think held her head down. It was then that a breeze caressed her face gently, turning her head. She was comforted, noticing the hand extended toward her. As she looked into the distance, she reminded herself of the young girl she once was, filled with such big dreams that it scared her. The years felt like the ocean waves she watched. One after another, they crashed. She always got her hopes up like that, only to have them crash into unseen rocks.

"Hope deferred makes the heart sick."
- Proverbs 13:12[NLT]

Isn't that why she settled for survival? The tears streamed down her face; her vision blurred by tears. The freezing force of the incoming wave took her by surprise, the freedom of surrender. As she opened her mouth, a quiet sound came forth. She tried again and again until she shouted. In place of bitterness, lonely tears of discouragement turned into tears of deliverance and bubbling laughter of delight.

"I am willing," she whispered, "I am willing."

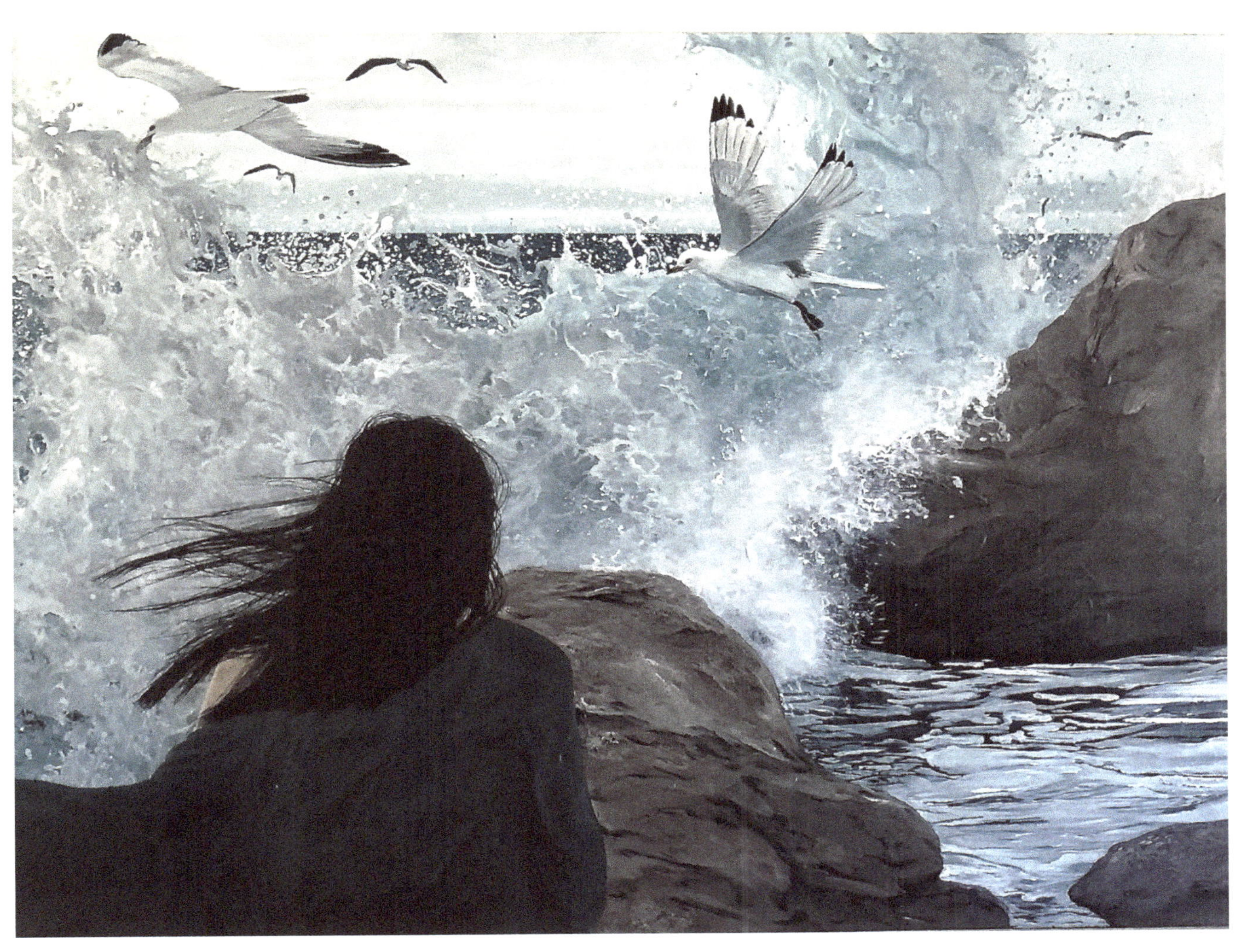

"We All Carry Something"

Each of us is uniquely created. No life is like another. We experience heartache and happiness differently. We were never promised that we wouldn't encounter many storms. However, the promise we do have is that we'll be given the strength to fight through the pain, an internal force to withstand even the worst storms. When we have this clarity, we know that the weather of our situation is not determined by simple luck. The weather itself is of no value.

When we were young and fearless, we loved exploring, learning, and taking risks. We were not hindered by the burdens yet to come. Once we grow up, these moments are replaced with the scars of painful experiences. We think of all the decisions we could've made better and the lives we could've changed. There will come a moment where you have to decide to exchange beauty for ashes. You cannot have both of them.

Can we live in forgiveness yet not forgive? Can we embrace confidence without giving up rejection? Can we embrace healing and not reject the hurt? Can we make progress towards our purpose and not give up bad habits of a wasted lifestyle? It's draining to oscillate, a painstaking process to give up on one and embrace the other.

We face crossroads in our lives that force us to make a decision. The comfort zone is somewhat reassuring, a delusion that you can control outcomes. This choice to accept the new will require attention, devotion, and prayer. You cannot wallow in self-pity and expect to be powerful. I could recount all the ways people have hurt, misjudged, or verbally abused me, but I made up my mind. Daily, I choose forgiveness, facing the days that come with expectancy.

"Forgetting what IS behind and reaching forward to what IS ahead."
- Philippians 3:13[HCSB]

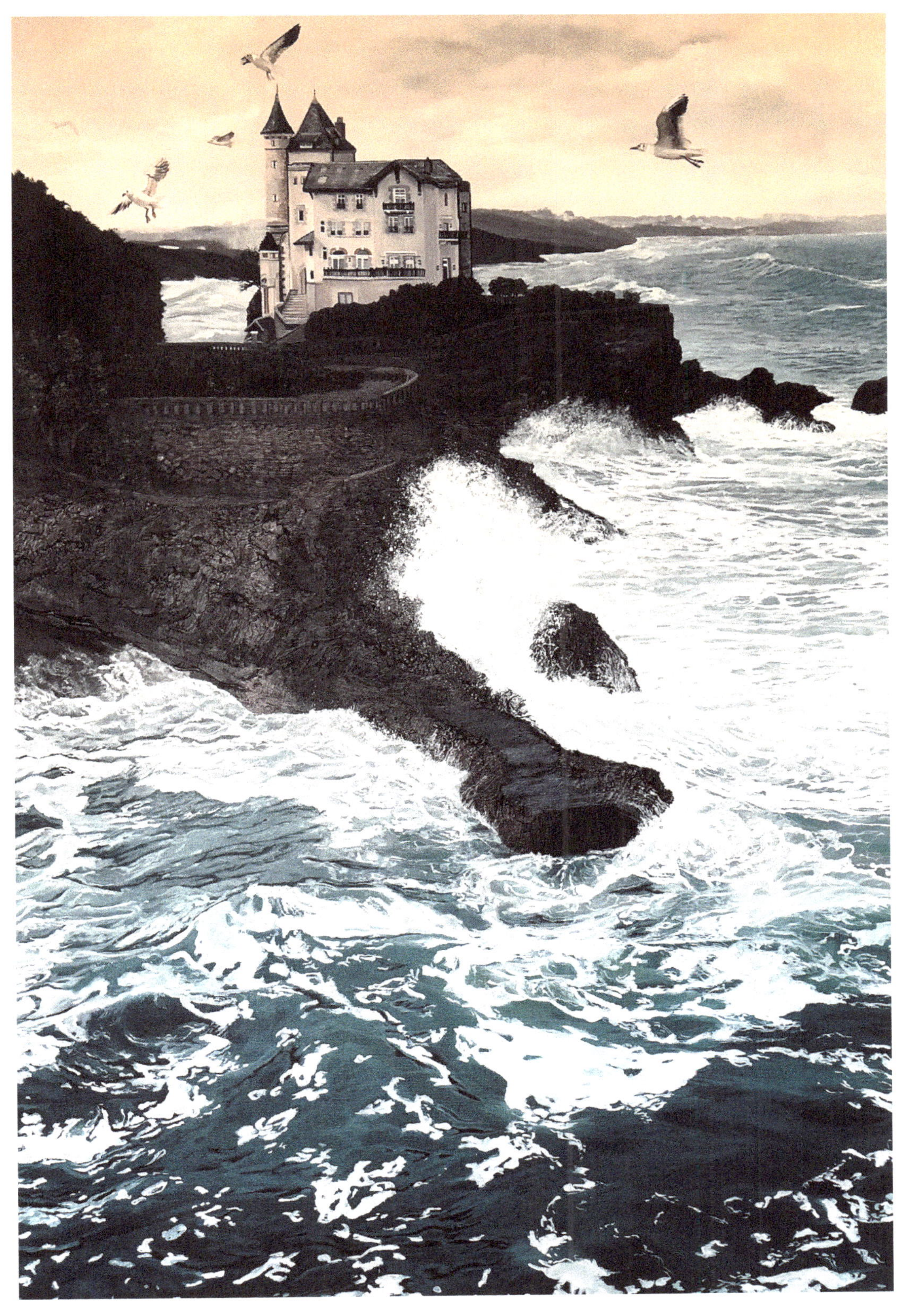

"Forward"

She was wearing a pair of outdated shoes. Centuries ago, they were in style; people used to get them in trades. But in the present, everyone stared. She could not control the reaction of those noticing her. "Let them look," she thought. The woman knew she was being watched and scrutinized. She fought tears as she heard their harsh remarks and whispers behind her back.

Though they spoke words of venom, at the same time, they were drawn to her kindness, talent, and generosity. Her words of comfort for the lonely and brokenhearted and the good counsel to those needing direction were highly regarded.

If only they would've known the truth. The shoes were the secret. She walked the rough places with confidence and never once lost her footing. "Be meek and humble," she was told, "But don't speak up unwanted. Don't share unnecessary information."

Those who were shrewd tried to make an offer for the shoes; they offered status and anything that could please the eye or excite the flesh. But isn't that how it all started? *Lust of the flesh, lust of the eye, pride of life?* Intellect and popularity were attractive, but she knew what it meant to take the shoes off. It took sacrifice and discipline to learn how to walk in them. She noticed how the shoes would glow a little brighter each time she overcame a temptation or battle. It encouraged her.

The shoes took her on the narrow path; it seemed like they knew the way. She saw people on the path turn back barefoot. Not everyone was willing to put down the heavy yoke. Some put it down just to take it again because they were unwilling to denounce their agreements with the pleasures of this world. But she kept on walking, even through the muddy swamps of discouragement and discontentment. Her Guide was with her; she felt the comfort and peace of His presence.

When asked if the shoes were worth that much, she would answer, "They are worth my life and everything I live for. They have a name and carry something special. They are the shoes of the Gospel of Peace."

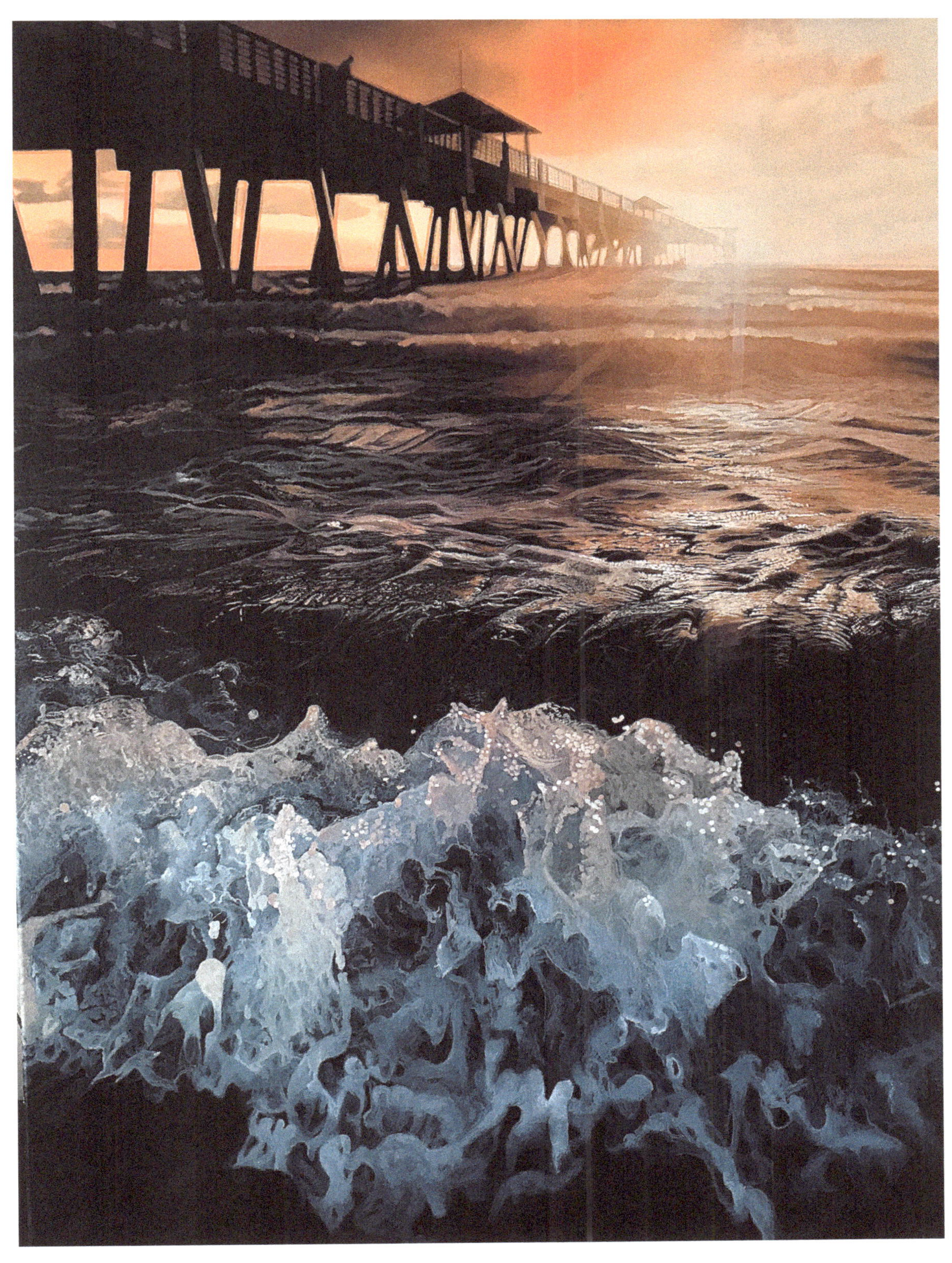

"Above All"

Today is an opportunity. It's a good day to touch the hand of your loved one, to unfold that treasured memory, to take the offered help. To appreciate that phone call. To reply to that message. To sit back and take the beauty of life in.

I never thought that I would have the privilege of getting to know benevolent people who have made a tremendous difference in my life. They think of others more than they think of themselves, finding what it means to be truly free. They own but do not let things own them; they lavishly give. Unfazed by rumors and gossip, they avoid worthless and foolish talk. They are the kind of people who hold the door for you when you have your arms full, who give you a cup of cold water on a hot day. They enrich others in their poverty. They choose to live in forgiveness, even when it's not their fault. They keep their promises, choose joy, and refuse to live offended.

Most of us, if we are honest, don't want to think of struggles. We don't welcome hardship, and we run away from challenges. We stay away from people who need us to go the extra mile for them. We are impatient because others have been impatient with us.

Or we give everyone grace except ourselves, thinking we are too far gone and push anyone away trying to get close to us. The walls of privacy are a refuge, a place of safety. It's not enough to be told that you can trust people because the ones you can trust are rare treasures. They come once in a while in your life, but if you don't take a chance to discern a friendship rooted in truth and honesty, you will never know.

What makes life beautiful? Is it pleasure and possessions?

What makes life meaningful? No pain, responsibilities, or sacrifice?

Isn't it true that a view is more beautiful from the top? If everything were leveled, there would be no reason to work or look forward to anything. If there are no valleys, there is no mountain to climb. Without the need to climb, you will not find the victory of the mountaintop. We can reach heights from where we can look back over the path we have come and sing a song of triumph on this side of heaven.

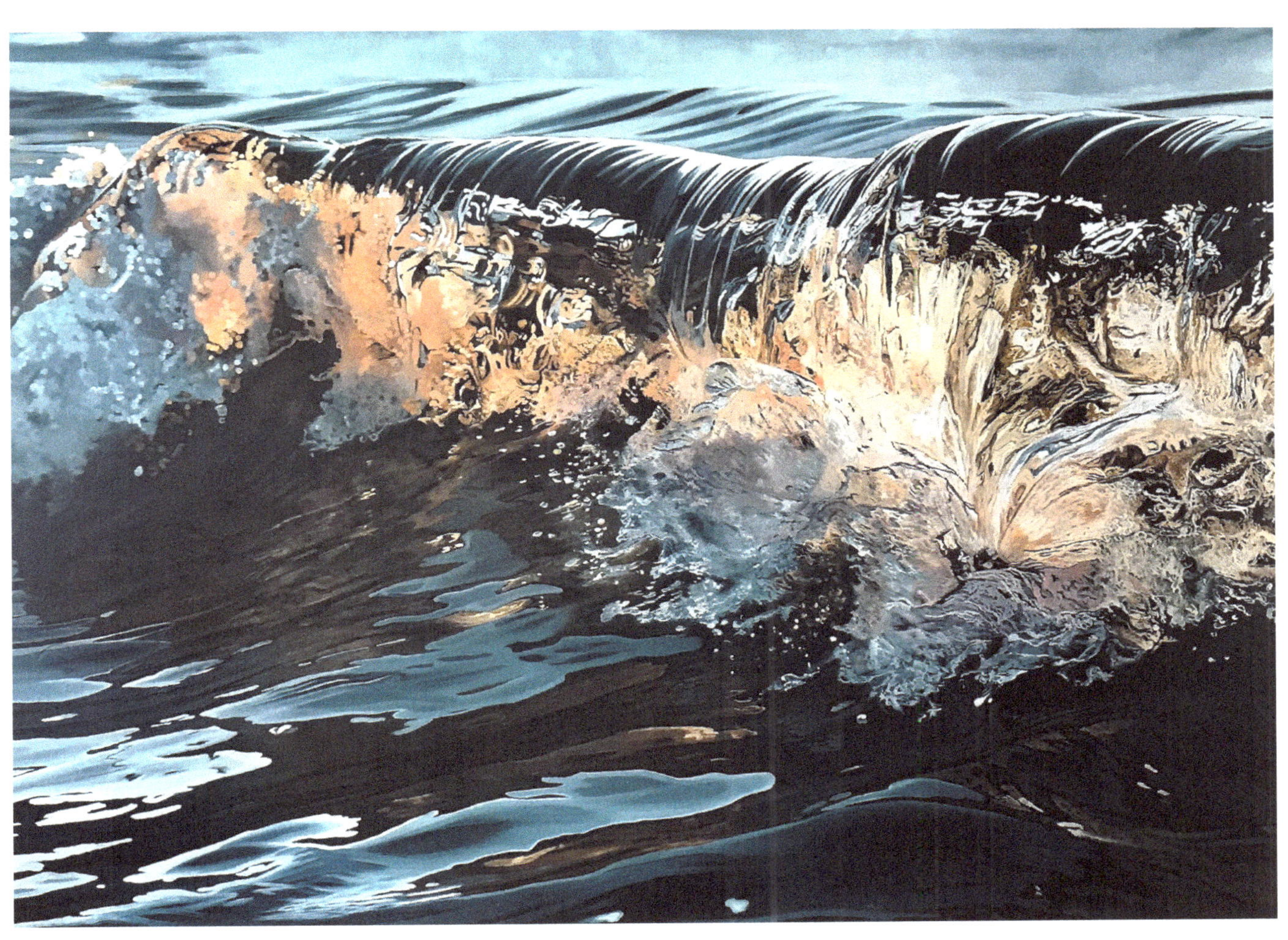

"It Is Time"

Recognition and Surrender, his most recent projects, were set upon easels in the studio. Taking a break, the painter left the paintings alone.

Recognition began as soon as the master left, though it did not realize he could still overhear. "Why is it that He works more on your canvas than on mine? Today, he barely turned his head to look towards me."

Surrender waited a bit, feeling a bit guilty that the master gave her so much attention. "It might be because you are so beautiful already. You have so much light. But look at me, I already have so much detail and still can't be compared to you."

Dejected, she continued, "I'll just be one of those nostalgic paintings—nothing special, just something that no one will truly like or appreciate. Everyone wants something warm and inviting to bring good memories back. Look at the sun shining on your horizon. It makes the waves look like liquid gold. You are going to be a masterpiece, one of his most treasured works that display the beauty of our master."

Recognition, quite pleased, said, "In truth, I was wondering why he spent so much time on you. It seems that no matter how much he works on you." Stopping for a moment, not sure how to continue, she whispered. "I saw him brushing off tears on his cheeks while working on you. He seemed somber when he worked on certain areas: the bend in the road with the rocks and pebbles, the rushing spring, the distant mountains. You look like autumn to me."

Surrender quietly responded, "Indeed, I think so too. The clouds in the distance seem wrapped in thick darkness, and the jar of heaven tilts to let the parched ground receive the needed rain. What is autumn? Is it just a season of colder days, darker skies, misty mornings, and falling leaves? In truth, what's so special about it?"

They heard the master's voice in the quiet. Moonlight shone through the studio.

"Light comes at the price of that which produces it. A candle must burn to give light. The path to tomorrow's glory is the DULLNESS of today. Recognition, at last, the glory revealed. Seen by all, desired by many, but only the Master knows the cost of such promise. The way to coronation is the crucifixion and the thorns before the crown. The light will shine brightest when the darkness IS deepest," he said.

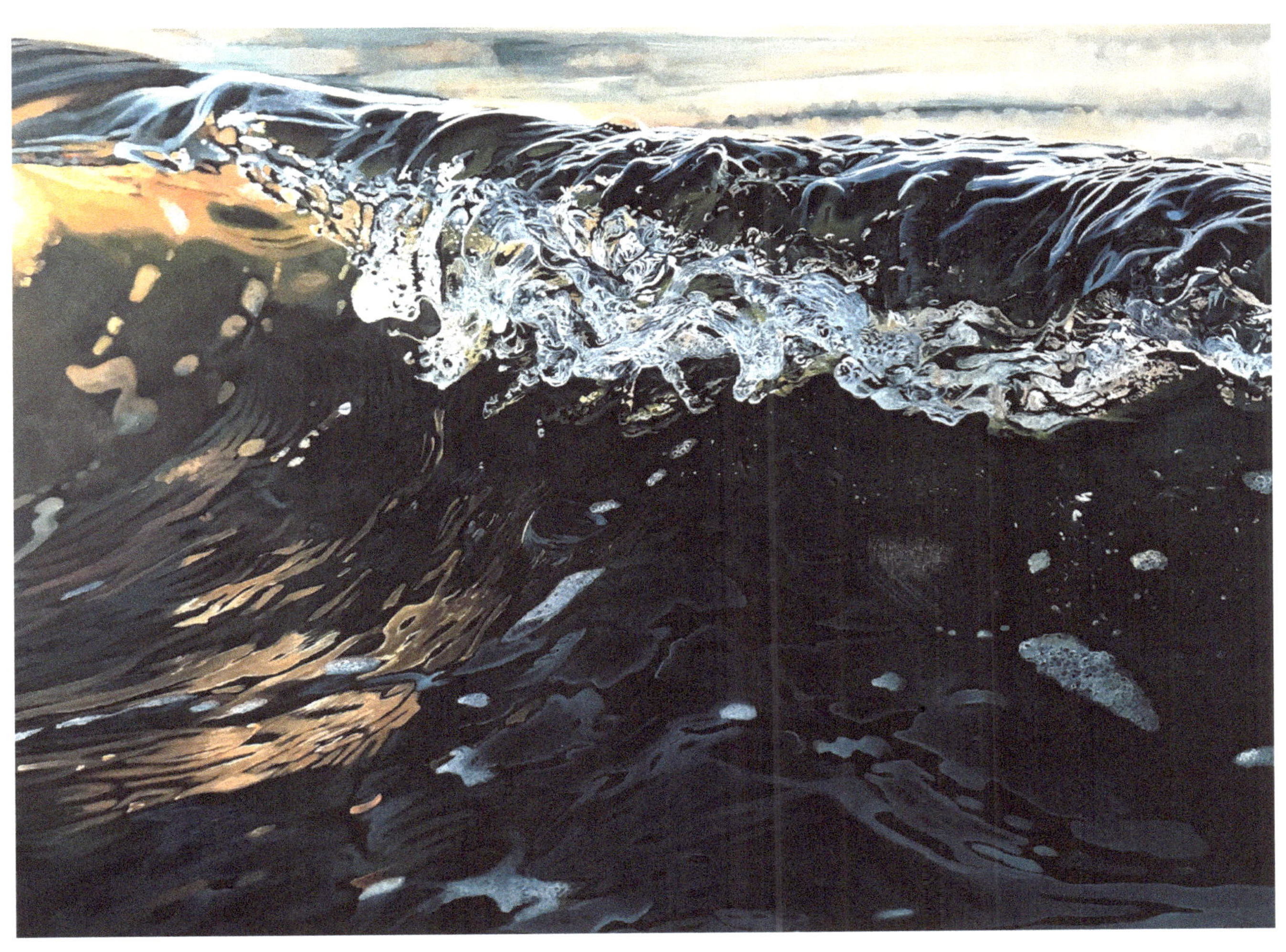

"Much More"

If I can throw a single ray of light,
Across the darkened pathway of another
If I can aid some soul to clearer sight
Of light and duty and this bless my brother;
If I can wipe from any human cheek a tear
I shall not have, then, lived in vain while here
If I can guide some erring to truth
Inspire within his heart a sense of duty
If I can paint within the soul of a rosy plant
A sense of light, a love of truth and beauty;
If I can teach one man that God and Heaven are near;
I shall not have, then lived in vain while here.
If from my mind I can banish doubt and fear
And keep my life attuned to truth, love, and kindness;
If I can scatter light and hope and cheer
And help remove the curse of mental blindness;
If I can make joy more, more hope, less pain
I shall not have lived in vain while here
If by life's road side I can plant a tree
Beneath whose shade some wearied head may rest
Though I may never share its shade or see its beauty
I shall yet be truly blessed
Though no one knows my name."

--ST FRANCIS OF ASSISI

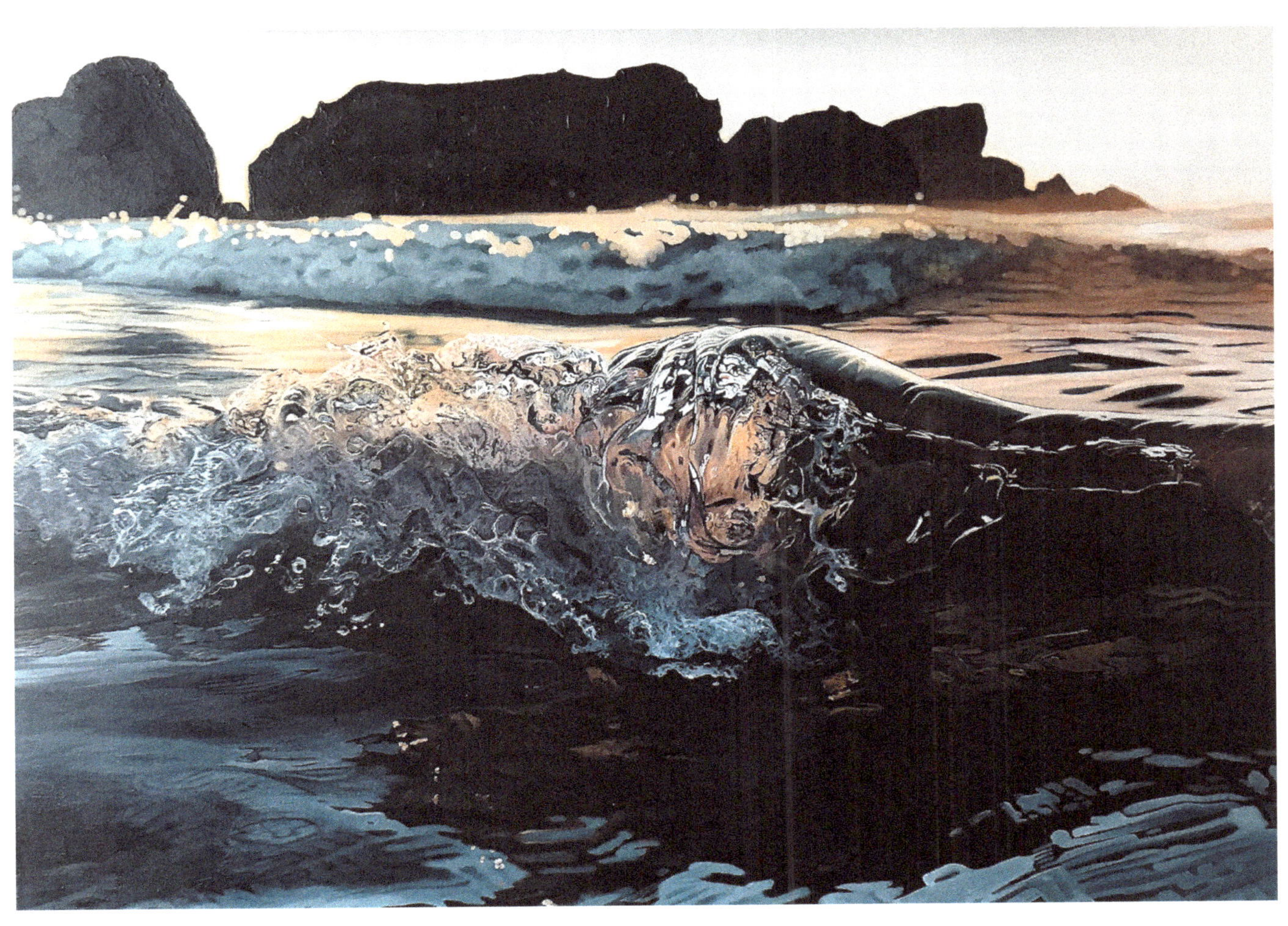

"If I Could"

Waiting takes patience, and patience is a virtue.

Waiting does not mean delay or an unkept promise; unless we are too lazy to invest in what we are entrusted with. From experience, I can say that nothing has tried me most in life than waiting—the minutes, hours, days, and years. We don't often find out why we had to wait so long for fulfilled desires, but we hear it said that everything worth having is worth the wait. It has gotten better over the years, as I learned from the process of creating. The small intriguing details require so much patience and attention. Progress comes in inches, not miles.

I can't say that I am a very patient person—I still have to stop myself from rushing the process or raising my voice—but I have gotten better by productively waiting. As I expect opportunities to come, I work towards getting better so that when the door I have waited for opens, I am ready. I can confidently walk through that door knowing I have what it takes. But what if you have given your best and yet, year after year of waiting, working, and trying your best, the open door doesn't come? What if an illness, a stolen opportunity by someone less qualified, or criticism comes your way?

Instead of seeing my potential, I have been told I am not ready for success and that I am just a starving artist. It's hard to see, trust, and move on without getting stuck. Especially when the days are monotonous and nothing extraordinary seems to happen. It's hard to believe that you are on the right path when met with these closed doors. It's so easy to settle for enough because we don't like waiting. Remember, waiting takes patience and is a virtue, but it is not absent of action.

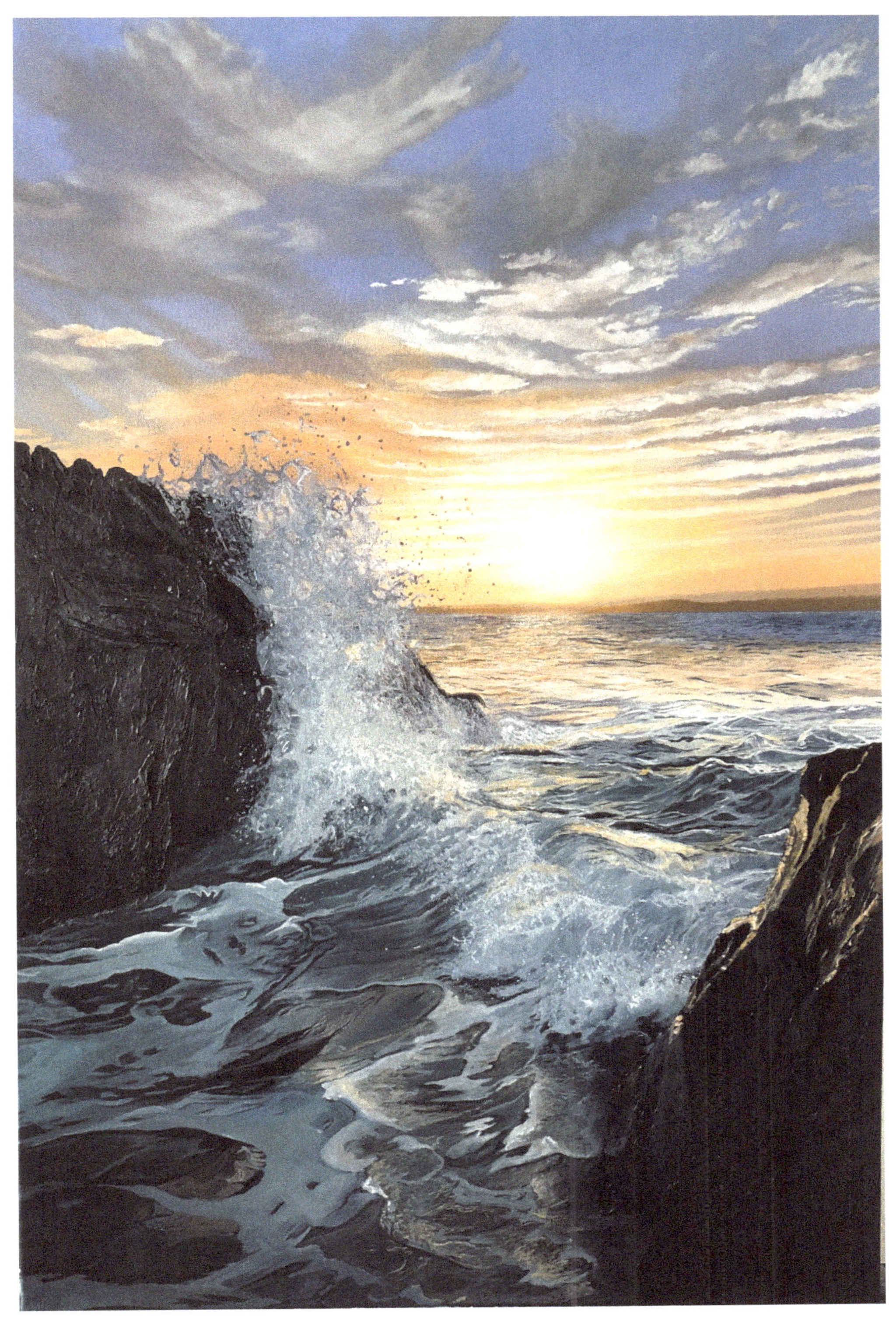

"Deep Calls To Deep"

Early morning walks are so refreshing and motivating. They are the best moments to contemplate the what-ifs and why-nots.

Her walks at the beach were her favorites. The waves seemed to caress the shore's face gently. A small delicate shell caught her attention as her feet sunk into the damp sand. Bending to pick it up, she noticed how alike it was to her, while still so different in size, shape, and texture.

As she walked, she put this shell with those she had previously gathered. She looked at the handful of shells, realizing the one that caught her attention the first time seemed more special than the others. What made someone extraordinary was the "extra"—extra work, extra effort, extra devotion, extra love. Just like people, the shell was unique in its gifting. *What makes someone more special than the rest?* She washed her hands in the warm water, letting the rest of the shells go. She noticed how the rest were pulled under the water where she couldn't see them again.

If people took the time to discover and work their gifts, the cemetery wouldn't be the wealthiest place on earth. Books would've been written, clothes made, homes repaired, songs sung, paintings painted, and lives changed.

It takes practicing something every day to get better at it, even though repeating the same thing can be boring or doesn't seem to pay off. That's how she created each piece. Even when she didn't feel like it, she painted. Even when tired or frustrated over making mistakes, she continued to persist.

There is no magic formula; it is simply a matter of putting in the work each day. A small amount of progress is still progress. It adds up every time.

Walking along the sand, she remembered why painting water was so unique to her.

Water is beautiful and satisfying, so delicate yet so strong. It can fill any crevice and can cover any surface. In its purest form, it is not harmful and satisfies the world's thirst. While cleansing and relaxing, it can bring turbulence and terror in its powerful currents. Unpredictable, water is much like life. Circumstances can make us soar high and feel undefeated and can just as quickly bring us to our knees and make us realize we are weaker than we think we are.

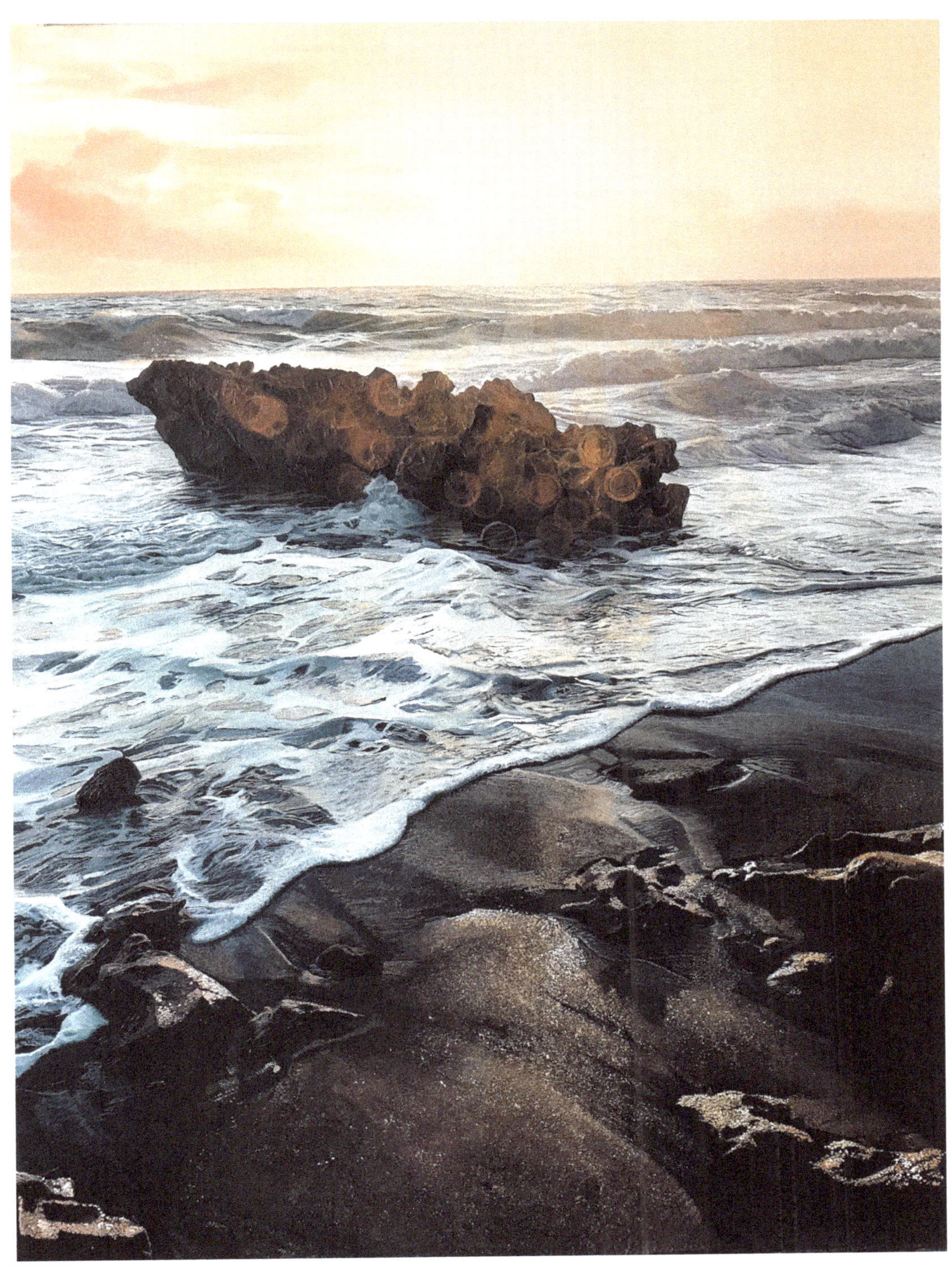

"Set Apart"

She was in a hurry. She wanted to do this fast before she changed her mind. She decided she would hide it in the attic, never to look at it again. She quickly jammed everything into a box: brushes, jars, colors, canvases, papers, and pencils. She was weary as she walked away. She worked hard but could no longer see it anymore, blinded by discouragement. Its cold, empty arms touched her dropping shoulders, sending shivers through her fragile state.

Maybe it was time to stop. Maybe it was just given for just a season. Perhaps she had had enough. The doubts swirled like tumultuous waves in a storm.

Not long after, she ran up the stairs again. Her hair, soaking up the tears running down her face, blocked her vision. She stumbled on the last step. Shakily moving closer to the box and opening it, the contents spilled across the floor. Looking at the mess around her, another outburst of frustration followed. The drawings scattered at her feet seemed to stare back at her. She tried to imagine a life without the gift that took so much space in her heart—she couldn't. The empty canvas next to her, surrounded by colors and brushes, seemed so inviting.

She bent down, face touching the cold floor, and she whispered a prayer. "Not today." Louder, she repeated, "Not today." At once, she felt strong arms around her frame—the warmth defrosting the icy touch of doubt. The place felt like holy ground.

She picked up the brushes, and she began something on the empty canvas that looked like a self-portrait. This time, it was focused on who she knew she was rather than what was seen. The image was of a girl who avoided the ordinary, motivated by a greater purpose. With strong beliefs and convictions, she held a deep desire for authenticity. Altruistic in nature, she pondered how her actions affected others. She was passionate about pursuing ideals and was willing to disrupt the status quo. Insightful, she had the uncanny ability to understand people's true motives, feelings, and needs.

She might sound perfect, but she was far from it. She was tedious and defined by idealism, defensive in the face of criticism and conflict. But she felt the need to live a life above reproach, a life of rare quality and excellence that was mirrored in her artwork. To her, each piece could easily still be a work in progress.

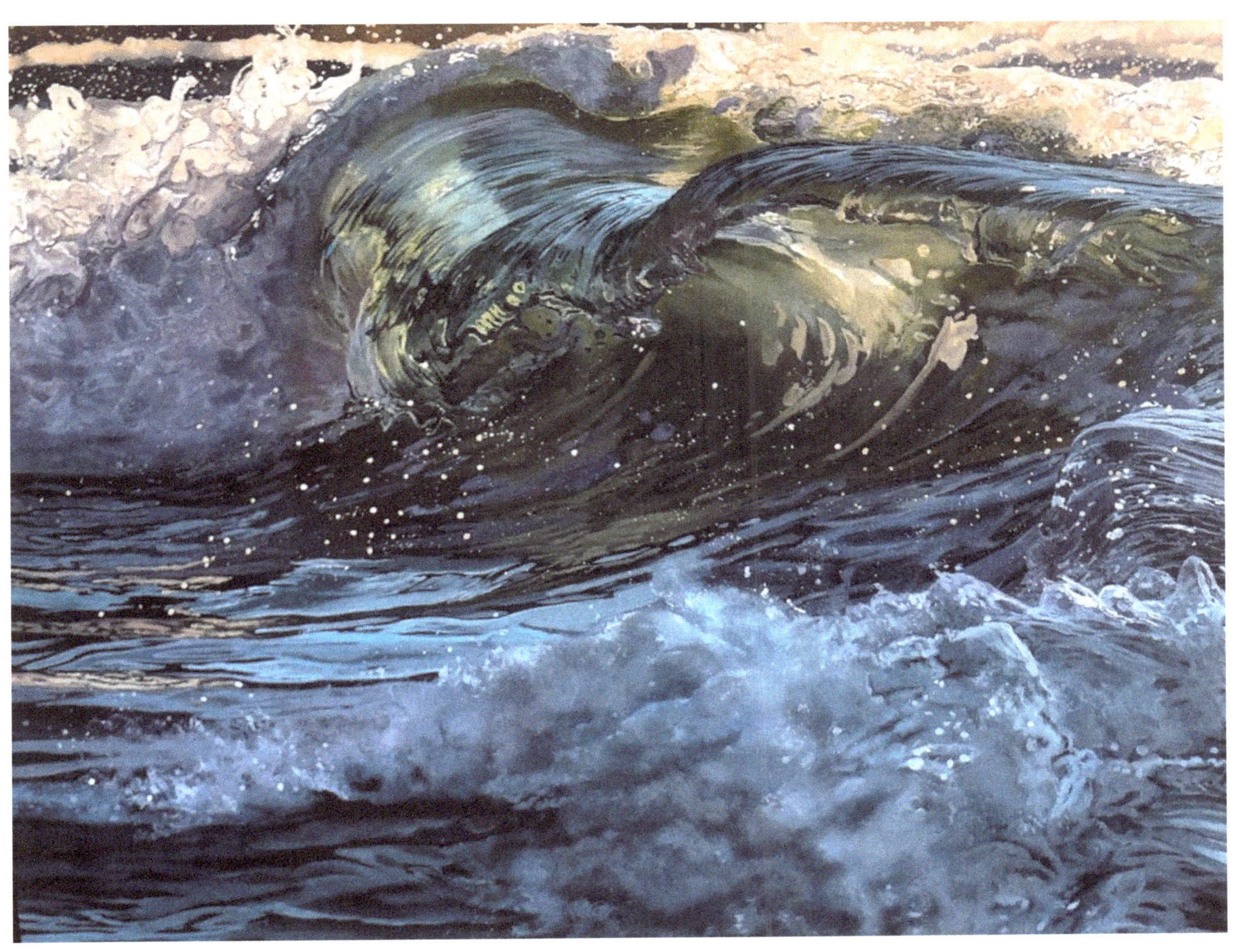

"Empathy"

"I can live alone, if self-respect, and circumstances require me so to do. I need not sell my soul to buy bliss. I have an inward treasure born with me, which can keep me alive if all extraneous delights should be withheld, or offered only at a price I cannot afford to give."

- Charlotte Bronte

She was enjoying a warm day at the park, barefoot on the grass. Summer days brought back childhood memories, days when she didn't feel like the world needed saving and wasn't so aware of other's needs. Growing up, she wanted to express herself, yet she couldn't put it into words. How could she explain how it felt to be an artist? Not even all artists are the same.

For sure, people have heard it said that artists paint what they feel; it's true. But so many have weird concepts about artists—that perhaps they try too hard to be original. Not everyone is this way. Some barely want to be noticed. As she looked down, she saw daisies peppered around the bench she now sat upon. Daisies, flowers that grow anywhere with well-drained soils and a lot of direct sun, reminded her of people who enjoy the spotlight and attention. Artists, however, are much like edelweiss, flowers that bloom in limestone soils upon mountain meadows of high altitudes. They grow in challenging environments.

It's intriguing to think of those wanting to be noticed who, when they are not, project their feelings onto others. They incorrectly assume those acknowledged wish to be known for their efforts in success when, in actuality, all they want is to keep doing what they are doing. She sometimes wondered why she was given this gift of art since it made her come out of her comfort zone and stand out. Laughing to herself, she reminded herself of the answer: creation takes courage, which requires stepping out of one's comfort zone. Art takes courage; to expose it takes courage. Every creative person is different in the way they create and express themselves. Don't think you know someone's reasons why they do what they do. It would be pleasant to find out that some want to help make the world around them a better place, even if it's just through art.

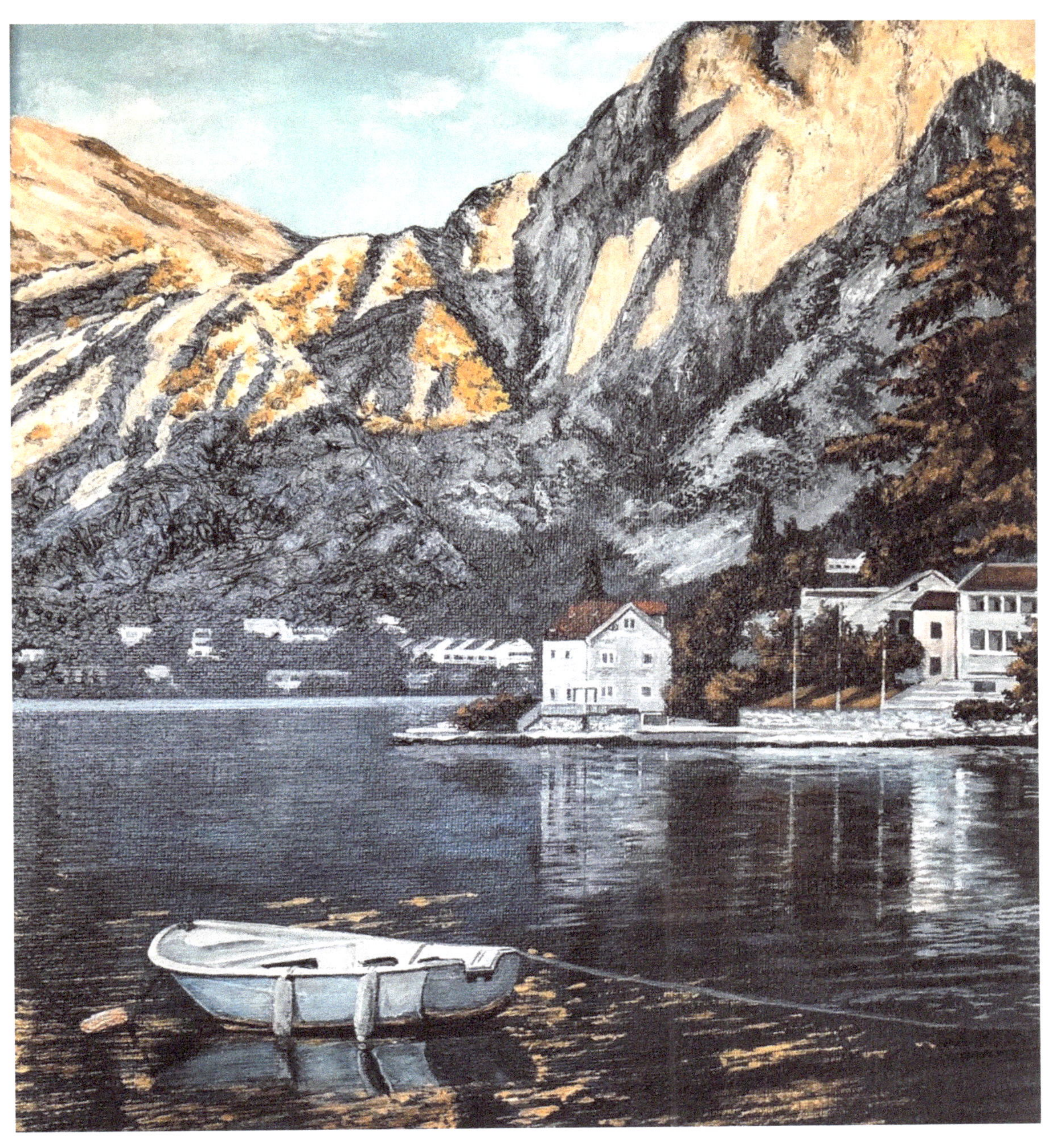

"Gratitude"

One can have all the skills, but they can only take them so far if they lack knowledge and understanding.

One step towards the results I was looking for, among other choices that lead to change, was investing in books. It is one thing to buy a book, but owning it has no meaning if it stays on your shelf gathering dust. To read it is one thing, but to understand and apply it is most important. I am pleased to say that I chose years ago to invest in understanding that which was beyond just knowledge. It takes understanding to make sense of the information you are receiving through knowledge. By applying this knowledge through understanding in decision-making, you gain wisdom. To invest in understanding is to prepare yourself, not just by buying books but by using them.

Don't be so poor that all you have is wealth. Learn to read, and you will start to love it. The secret of living a rich life is not owning material things. Even if I were to entrust you with great riches, you would waste it all without understanding why it was given to you. Your mind needs to be transformed. Just because someone has wealth doesn't mean they are wise. Wealth can be inherited, but mental wealth requires work. Lack of knowledge closes doors that your giftings can open, but it's vital to pay attention to your words and mental process to step through the door. You can take many things from me, but you cannot take away my freedom to think for myself. You can try to make me feel bad for many things, but if my mind is a fortress—well-guarded and protected—you cannot make me hate, despise, or return evil. That is why it's crucial to choose what information we put into our minds. Learning takes time, just like a seed takes time to grow into a tree. It's a process. However, the seed of knowledge planted in the soil of understanding will produce the fruit of wisdom.

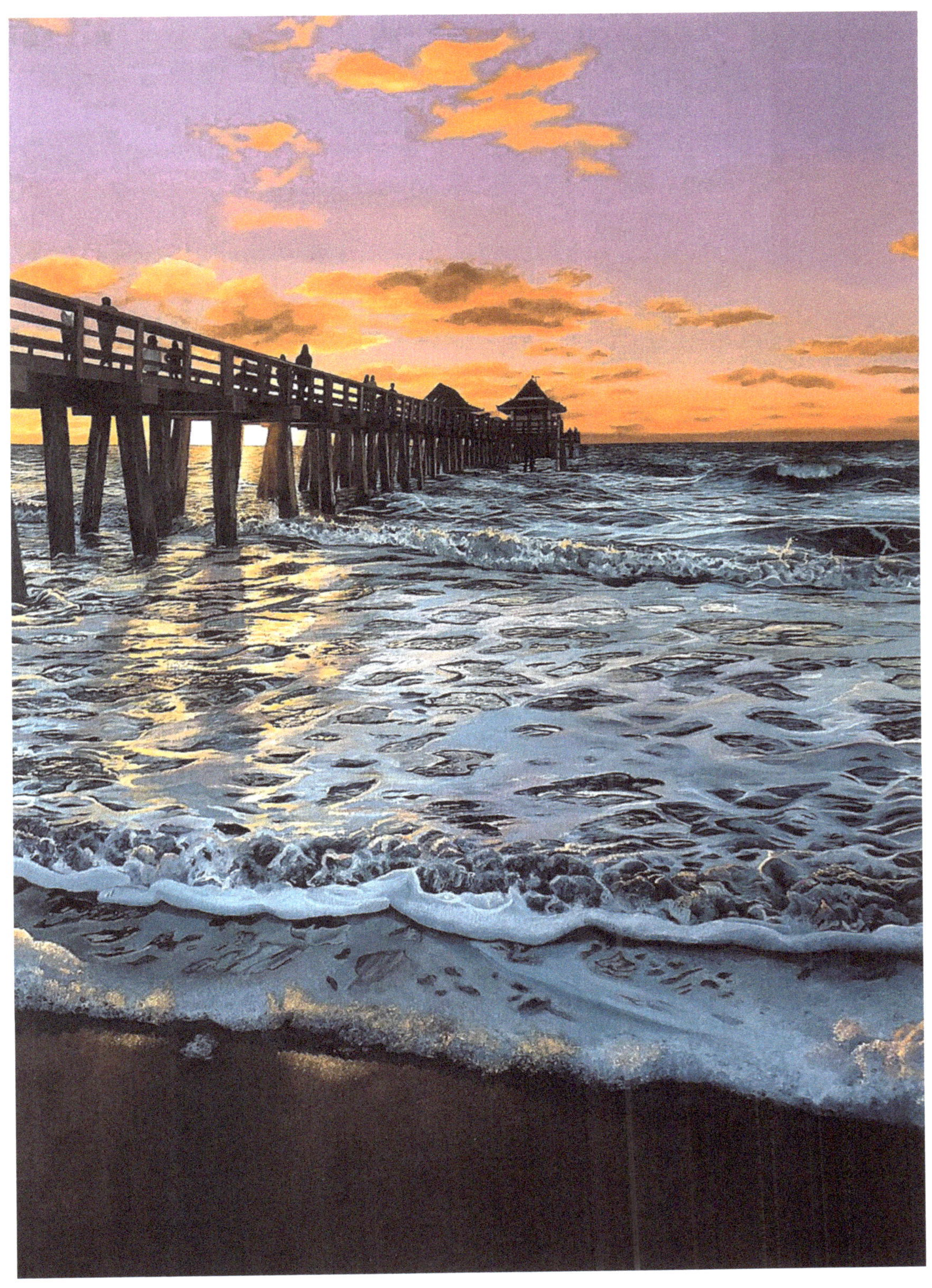

"Knowledge"

hu·mil·i·ty, noun

/hyü-ˈmi-lə-tē/

: freedom from pride or arrogance

I look for it. I hear it's hard to find. At times, I feel like I'm looking for it in the wrong faces. It should be in certain places, yet it's portrayed in unexpected faces. Some think they have it; some are aware that they don't, and others desire to obtain it. Once you have it, you don't realize it. If you were to acknowledge it, it would shy away from the spotlight. When you have it, you appreciate a compliment for what it is without thinking of it too much. It brings you to a state of mind in which you can appreciate the masterpiece you've created, take pleasure in that as much as you would if another had done it, and rejoice gratefully in your abilities and gifting as in your neighbor's.

It fascinates me, the mystery that it is. It comes unobserved, leaving the moment you notice it. It's pure, lovely, gentle, and radiant. It blossoms unobserved. It's the rarest thing I have seen, the most ardent thing I desire. I yearn to see it in the people I admire. What astounds me is that it has the power to bring you the greatest honor and makes space for you in unexpected places.

Humility, to me, it's the virtue of all virtues—the one I long to embrace and possess. It cannot be bought with treasures or traded for riches. The one who obtains it is the wealthiest of all without knowing. The owner—the One who is omniscient, omnipotent, and omnipresent—knows it well. He owns and holds all things. His breath gives and takes away. He is the possessor of all gifts; He shared them without repentance. Confidently, with perfect love and humility, He restrained Himself so we can partake and partner together. Having all of heaven, He left it behind to step into humility—serving when He should be served. Humility is the image I long to bear, the image of my Creator.

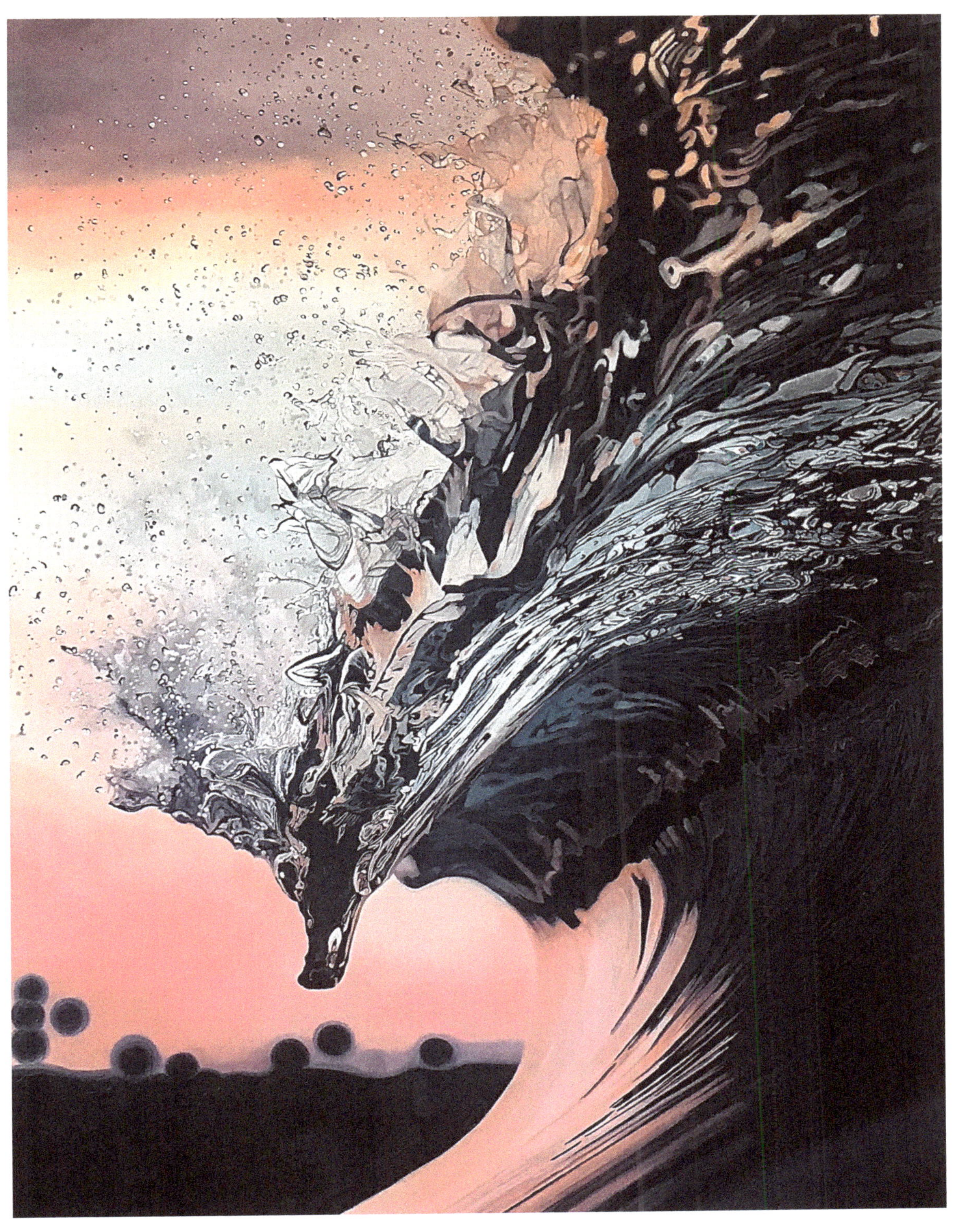

"Humility"

I *prayed for Peace...* What came my way looked like anything but that.

Looking up in frustration, I questioned how this could be. "This is not peace; adverse winds blew like a tempest through the night. It is not the news of grief and sorrow, strife and tension. Where is the commitment? Why is there doubt and fear?" As restlessness increased, I bowed my head and let my heart cry out. "Alas, I cannot bear this any longer. I ask for Peace."

His firm voice seemed to have come from behind, but it was before me as He spoke to the storms in my life to be still. At once, the winds and waves obeyed. Soft rain showers smoldered the fiery trial, like fireproof armor against which heat is powerless. A feeling of serenity followed the storm.

Didn't He say, *"Peace I leave with you. My peace I give to you. I do not give to you as the world gives. Your heart must not be troubled or fearful" John 14:27 [HCSB]*

My eyes were opened. I understood that when He sends peace, no one can disturb it—not lack, condemnation, or difficult people. Through everything that He has allowed to come my way, there is the assurance that He will never leave nor forsake me. He is the only One that keeps His promise.

"Then you will experience God's peace, which exceeds anything we can understand.
His peace will guard your hearts and minds as you live in Christ Jesus."
- Philippians 4:7[NLT]

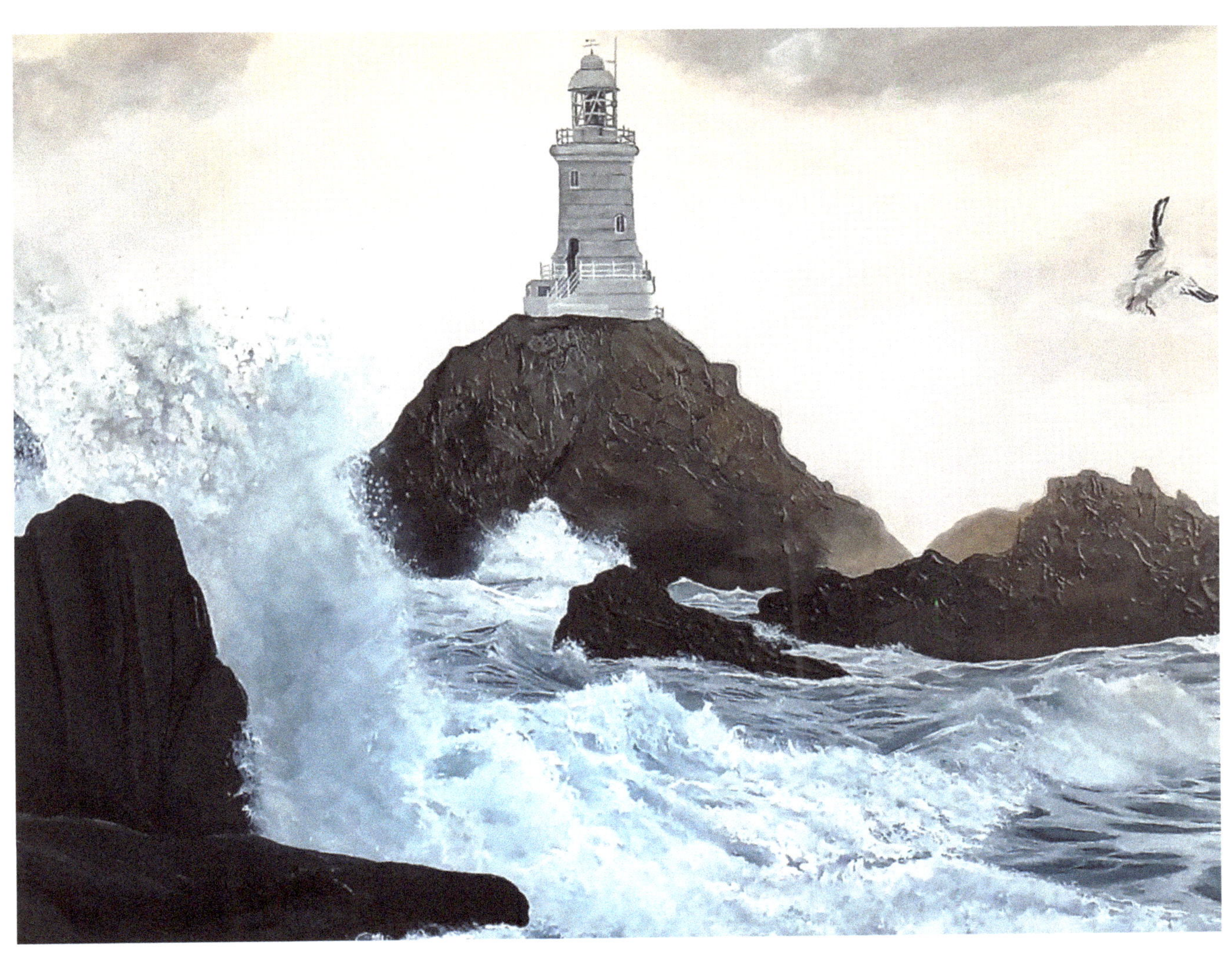

"Shalom"

"Love is patient, love is kind. Love does not envy, is not boastful, is not conceited, does not act improperly, is not selfish, is not provoked, and does not keep a record of wrongs. Love finds no joy in unrighteousness but rejoices in the truth."
- 1 Corinthians 13:4-6[NLT]

Can you wait patiently through the years of prayers that don't seem to be answered?
Can you be kind to the people who cut you in a line?
Can you appreciate what someone has without being envious of it?
Can you enjoy your life and gifts without being boastful?
Can you appreciate compliments without becoming conceited?
Can you be proper even when no one you know is around?
Can you share your blessings and not be selfish?
Can you be patient with demanding people and not be provoked?
Can you look over a dishonor done to you without keeping a record of wrong?
Can you stand against wickedness and not rejoice in unrighteousness?

"[Love,] it bears all things, believes all things, hopes all things, endures all things."
- 1 Corinthians 13:7[NLT]

Love bears: taking responsibility for those entrusted to you. It is to stay awake in the hospital holding their hand, working extra hours to provide for your family, or extending forgiveness to the crude guard at your prison cell.

Love believes: believing in the integrity of your loved ones. It is to trust that those working under you are being fair and true and not to be suspicious of everything coming through your door.

Love endures: the stamina required to run the difficult course. It is to keep going when adversity is running by your side. The testing of your faith produces endurance, which produces proven character. When perseverance has done its work, you have matured.

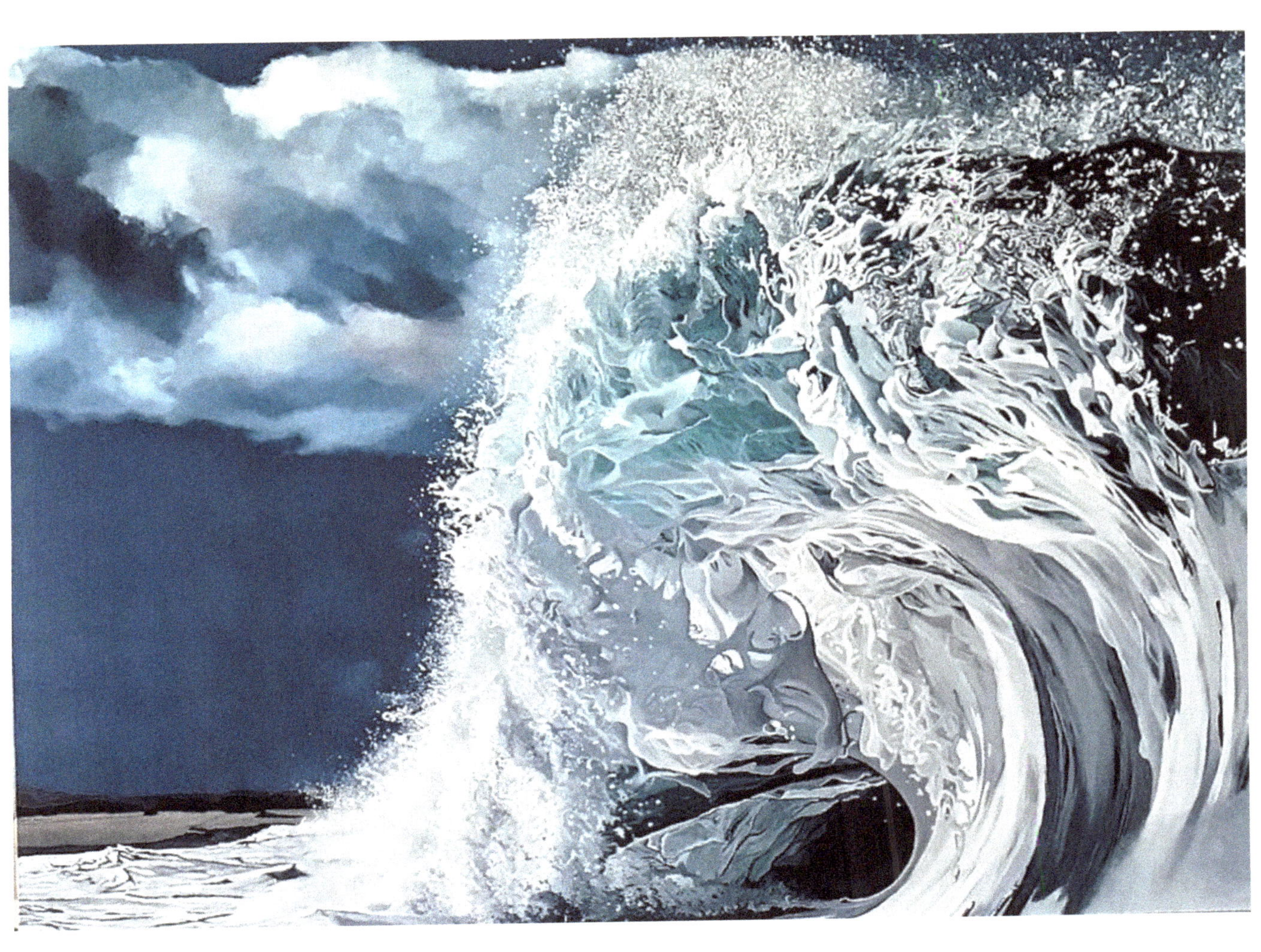

"But The Greatest Is"

Today, I searched my heart for its true motives.

I want to believe that I am a good person. I know I'm not the best, nor am I the worst. Why would I want to be kind, loving, compassionate, and generous? I could live an average life, but I believe with everything in me that we are all capable of so much more. Success would be about me, but significance about others.

We live in a world where things are done half-meant, half-known, half-delighted. We are afraid of dying to ourselves. We are fastened by fear, and our souls are captive in flesh tents. If we believed that people are not disposable and are eternal creatures, we wouldn't live like tomorrow won't arrive. In a world where parents don't get along, children are misunderstood, sisters hurt sisters, and brothers go against brothers, search your heart. When you do, you'll find that we are all capable of evil. We all have disobedience and pride within us that's why we need the truth of what we were created to become. It's not about us; it can't be that simple. We are not prepared because we don't want to give up lies. We don't want to give up sorrow for true joy. But can it be that by embracing the truth, we are required to change? We cannot leave the middle grey, living our lives half-heartedly. Is it hard to believe that Someone gave everything for us wholeheartedly?

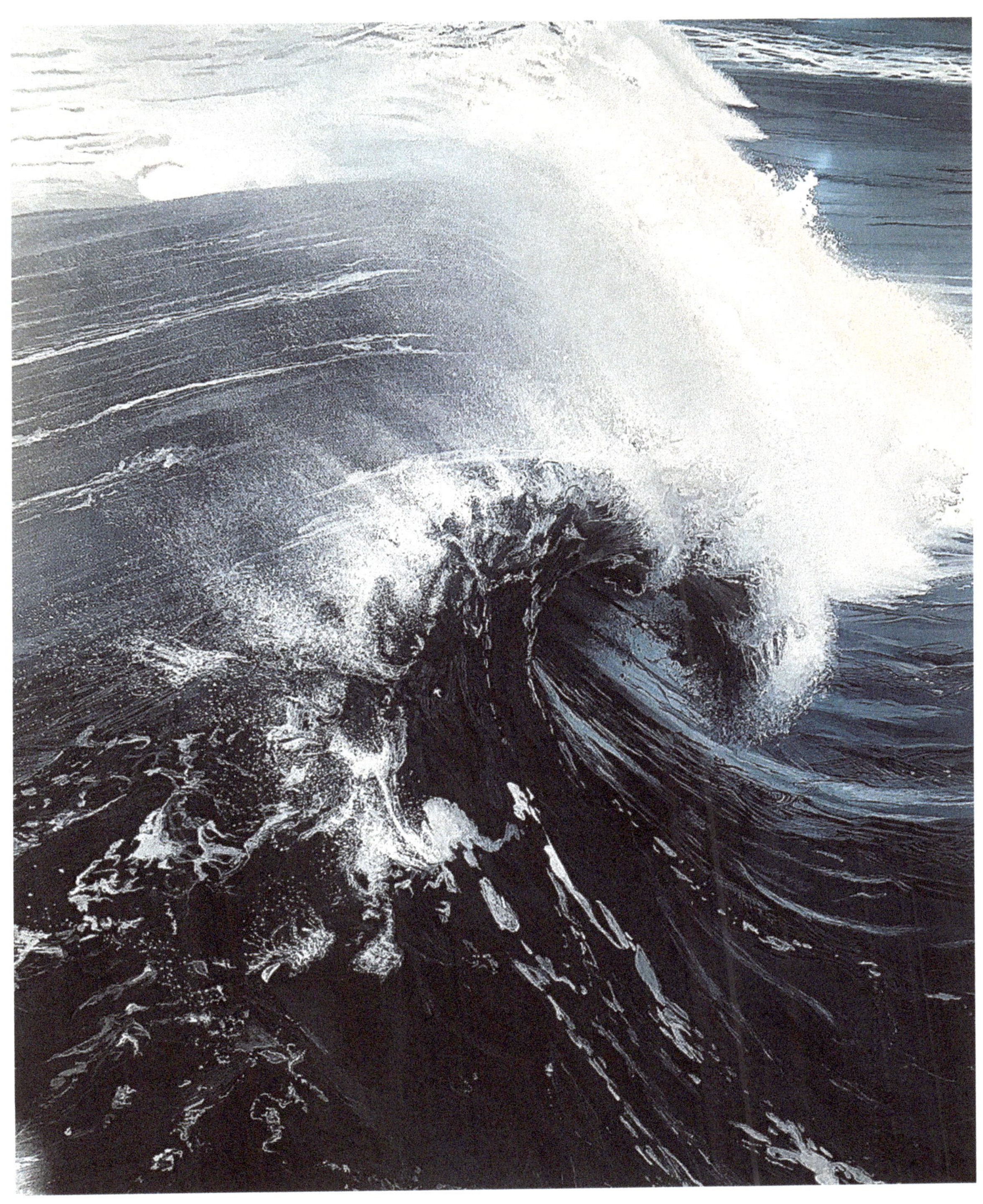

"Courage"

There was a deaf man who made it his goal to reach the top of a mountain, one that few dared to hike, and even fewer made it to the top. The trail to the top of the mountain took him through a village. The people in that village did not know he was deaf. While traveling through, the village people came out, calling out and beckoning him to rest. "Not everyone makes it to the to," some called out. "Most of the people go only halfway. Do you think you're an exception?" Because of his deafness, he believed he was being encouraged to continue. Moving through the village, he progressed.

Reaching halfway, he noticed an inviting cabin. Though he was exhausted, he knew that he had to push even harder to make it before nightfall. There was another cabin where he could rest at the top of the mountain. As he made up his mind to continue, the cabin door opened, and its inhabitants came out holding a cup of something that looked warm and delicious. Smiling, they called him to join them. Not understanding he was deaf, they called out to him more loudly. Again, he thought he was being encouraged to continue. He kept going, pushing harder than before.

At last, he made it. He looked out towards the valley and realized someone else was there. Next to him was a man of quiet confidence; his statue was commanding, although small and frail. The eyes that looked at him were full of love and compassion. He wasn't sure who this man was, but he had his respect. There was no need for words; his eyes communicated to him everything he needed to know.

On his way back, he thought about what he had learned from the stranger. He understood that it is not as important if one succeeds or fails, but more so that one at least tries. He had also learned that people may say it's impossible until it's done. Many pilgrims stop at the cabin of comfort and miss the view from the top. People will often discourage you, not because they want you to fail, but because they don't want to be challenged to change. Most say it can't be done until it is by someone unwilling to give up.

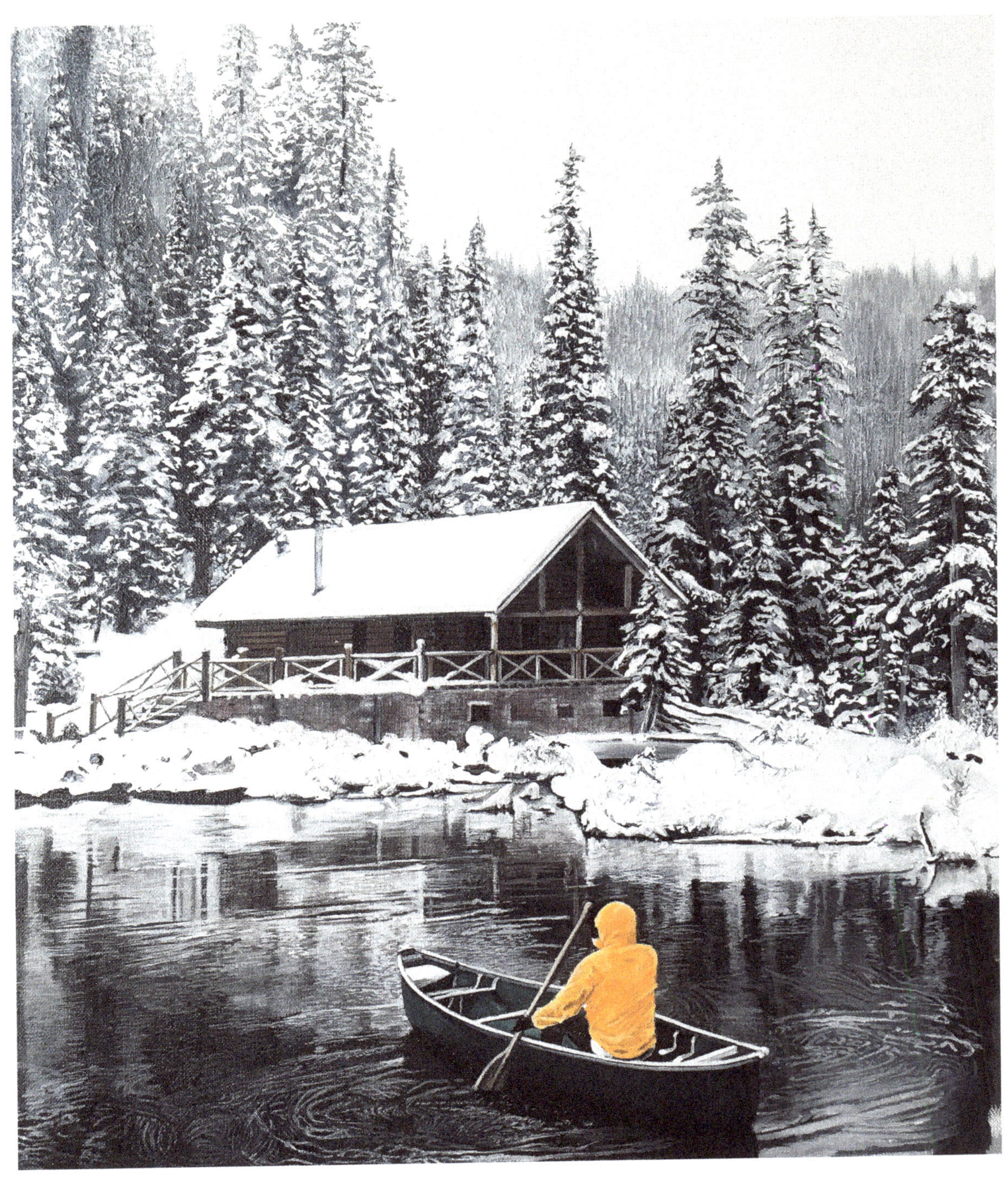

"Perseverance"

She wondered when she dozed off. Planning to take a short break in her recliner, she somehow had fallen asleep. walking to the kitchen, she put water to boil for a cup of tea. She tried hard to remember the dream. She always dreamed, but this one was different. Sitting down at the kitchen table, she closed her eyes and began to recall the image.

On a stage being applauded by many, she received crown after crown made out of glass. Contemplating what this meant, she realized how true it was to life. The praises of man were like these glass crowns. Without a head held high, it will slip and break. So beautiful yet fragile, these crowns will not last unless confidence, appearance, and success are maintained. If one stumbles, it is broken into pieces, just like the reputation of the one who once wore it. It doesn't matter how broken, uncomfortable, or flawed the wearer of feels; the crowd expects a performance. Every artist is first a person; they are more than their titles. They are praised for their talent and rewarded for their performance, not for putting their lives aside to help others. She wondered whose lives could they have changed but their own.

At the screeching of the kettle, she got up, walking back to the couch with her tea. Her mind trailed off to the true heroes: soldiers, firefighters, doctors, police officers, teachers, and parents. Those were people who made a difference in the world. We may never hear about the widows or orphans left behind for the heroes" actions. Who can call them by name, account for their sacrifice, or know the extent of their bravery?

"There is no greater love than to lay down one's life for one's friends."
- John 15:13[NLT]

She closed her eyes, remembering the rest of the dream. With curtains closed, she was alone. She recalled people telling her that death would not take the wise person by surprise because they were always prepared. She was told to look forward to a well done and unbreakable crown only given to those who had overcome.

she picked up a book tattered by time—the Holy Book, which was dear to her grandfather. Noticing a bookmark, she opened the page only to have the words take her breath away.

"The Master said, 'Well done, my good and faithful servant. You have been faithful in handling this small amount, so now I will give you many more responsibilities. Let's celebrate together.'"
- Matthew 25:23[NLT]

In the end, it will not matter how many awards we have won in the eyes of mere humans, but how well we lived the only life we were given.

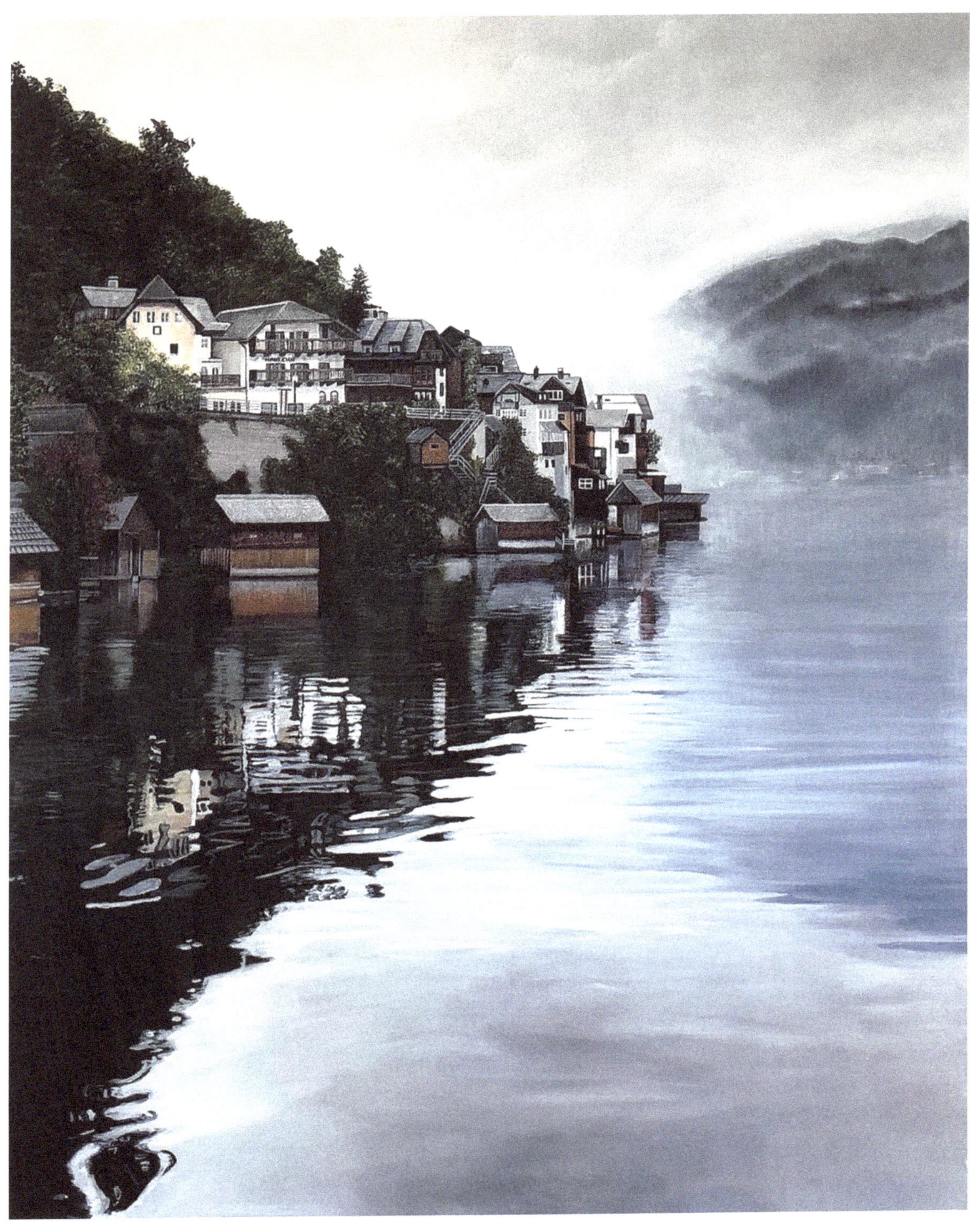

"Well Done"

Have you seen how a child trusts? A child, so pure and true, doesn't doubt after they ask. They take your word for it, believing you will keep your word if you promise something. That's why they are so expectant.

Have you seen how a child persists? When they lose something, they search until they find it, or they ask for help. They do not quit until they get it back.

We have so much to learn from children. They are persistent, curious, and hardly forgetful. They teach grown-ups how to laugh without pretense and take delight once again in the simplest of things.

"So anyone who becomes as humble as this little child is the greatest in the Kingdom of Heaven."
- Matthew 18:4 [NLT]

With childlike faith, we would have more prayers answered and more reasons to be thankful. Why are we told to become like a child? The young do not have evil intentions but hold minds full of innocence. They are not hindered by logic or intellect; they don't doubt the words of their parents. Unless we become more like little children, we cannot enter the Kingdom of Heaven.

We cannot accept the sacrifice made for us by logic, only by belief alone. As adults, we find ourselves trying to pay our way to heaven with good deeds and intentions. An adult thinks of all the ways they need to take care of loved ones while a child lives in the present. They won't worry about tomorrow—if they have enough food and clothing or a roof over their head—because they know their parents will take care of them.

"So don't worry about these things, saying, 'What will we eat? What will we drink? What will we wear?' These things dominate the thoughts of unbelievers, but your heavenly Father already knows all your needs."
- Matthew 6:31-32 NLT]

Unless we stop reasoning, trying to make sense of the sacrifice paid for us on the cross, and believe like a child, putting away the hindrances of intellect, we cannot embrace the Truth of Jesus' perfect sacrifice.

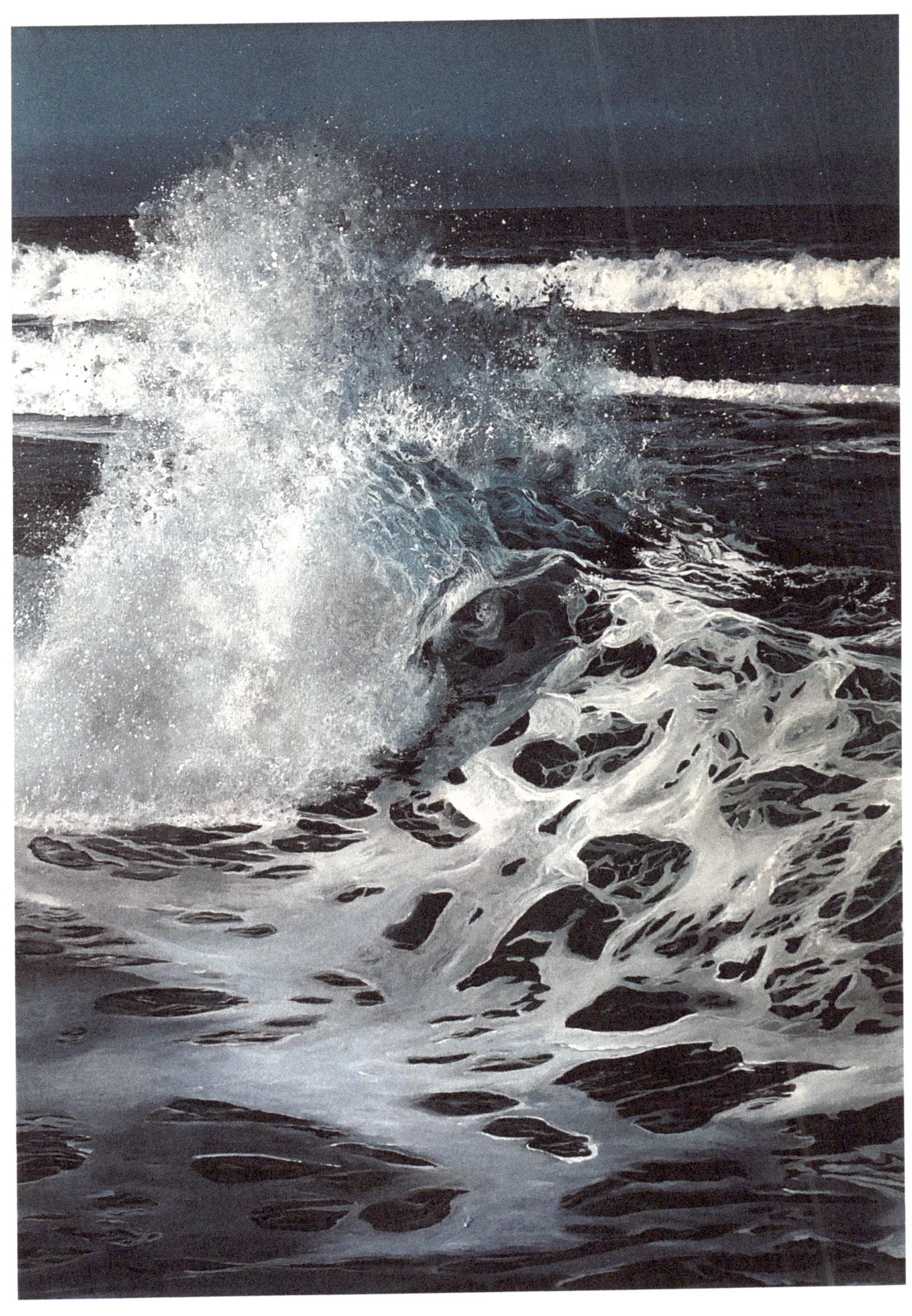

"Do Not Worry"

She was organizing when she found a box in her closet that she hadn't seen in a while. Dusting the thin layer of dust off the top of it with her hand, she opened it and sighed... *memories*. She had found her library of journals, lots and lots of them. While she flipped through pages, she began to laugh loudly. What nonsense she had written as a child. Journaling always made her feel better because she could write out her feelings and emotions. Or, at least, she tried.

Her face became somber as she came across a section of smeared pages. It was dated 20 years ago, but she remembered the years of high school like they were yesterday. Her beliefs made her different from her classmates. She couldn't figure out back then what made them bully and annoy her when she tried to be nice. False confidence made her look conceited, a mask she wore so they could not guess how she actually felt. She didn't want to be so defensive, but she felt she had to prepare herself for whatever would happen each day when she arrived at school. Wiping away tears gathering at the corner of her eyes, she couldn't remember a time in her life where she didn't feel different. She didn't think of herself as being more special. On the contrary, growing up, she felt very insecure because of how her peers treated and talked to her.

Their harshness stemmed from being bothered by her beliefs. That was what started the chain reaction between her classmates. Why would they be impertinent? Why would they care so much about what she believed? She only had strong morals; it didn't hinder what they chose to do. She decided to have no part in their activities because she knew they were wrong. She knew better.

Exhaling, she leaned on the wall and stretched her legs in front of her. She thought deeply about how a child is affected by what their parents teach them or let them watch. Anything can damage their innocence, influencing their perception of the world around them. What is said and done in a family will be mirrored in society by their children. While she didn't have children of her own yet, she hoped that hate would not be a burden she would inflict upon them when she did. No matter how different someone's beliefs are, she concluded there should always be boundaries of respect.

"TEACH A YOUTH ABOUT THE WAY HE SHOULD GO; EVEN WHEN HE IS OLD HE WILL NOT DEPART FROM IT."
- Proverbs 22:6[HCSB]

Looking back, she didn't have any regrets. At least she didn't respond to them in the same manner. She got up and, taking a handful of journals, threw them into the trash can. Feeling light, she walked away, reminding herself to forget their mistakes and remember the lessons learned.

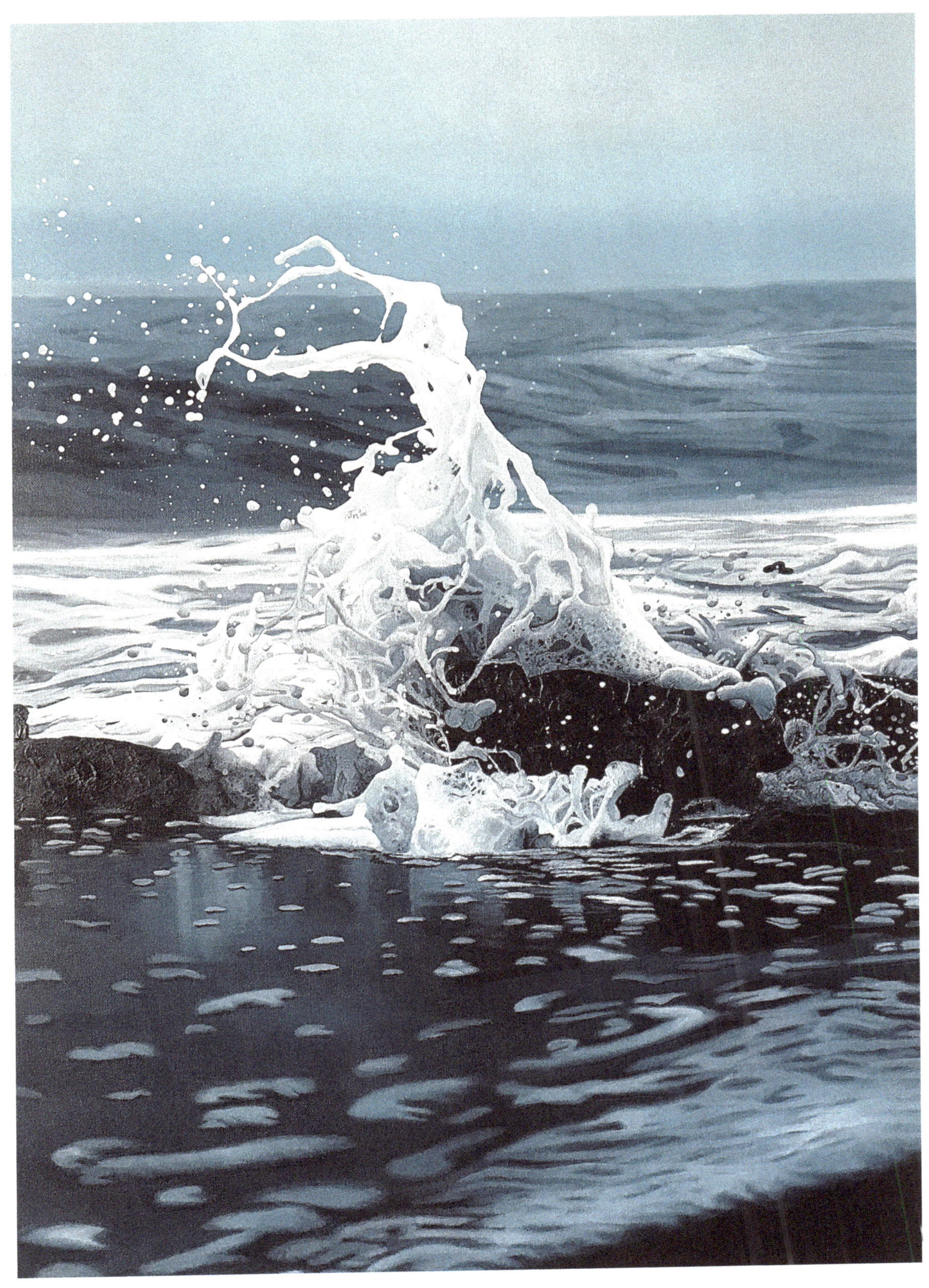

"Receptivity"

Yesterday... Yesterday is like a photo; you look at it in remembrance, but can't go back to change anything about it. It doesn't matter if you don't like how something turned out. Don't let your feelings be hindered by what you wish you could go back to fix.

Today... Today is like a painting in progress; you decide how to feel about it and choose what you let come your way. Do what you can with the tasks at hand, for you never know what you can accomplish.

Tomorrow... Tomorrow is like an unfinished puzzle; every day, we add another piece to it. Progress lets us make sense of our yesterdays. However, until the final piece is in place, we cannot see the whole picture. We can only see and understand in part.

"Now we see things imperfectly, like puzzling reflections in a mirror,
but then we will see everything with perfect clarity."
- 1 Corinthians 13:12[NLT]

Yesterday, we made promises. Today we make new decisions. Tomorrow, we might not keep them. But there is One who never changes.

"Jesus Christ is the same yesterday, today, and forever."
- Hebrews 13:8[HCSB]

He operates outside time and space; our circumstances and moods do not move Him. He is the only One who can promise something that seems too good to be true. So, dare to trust Him. Dare to ask Him.

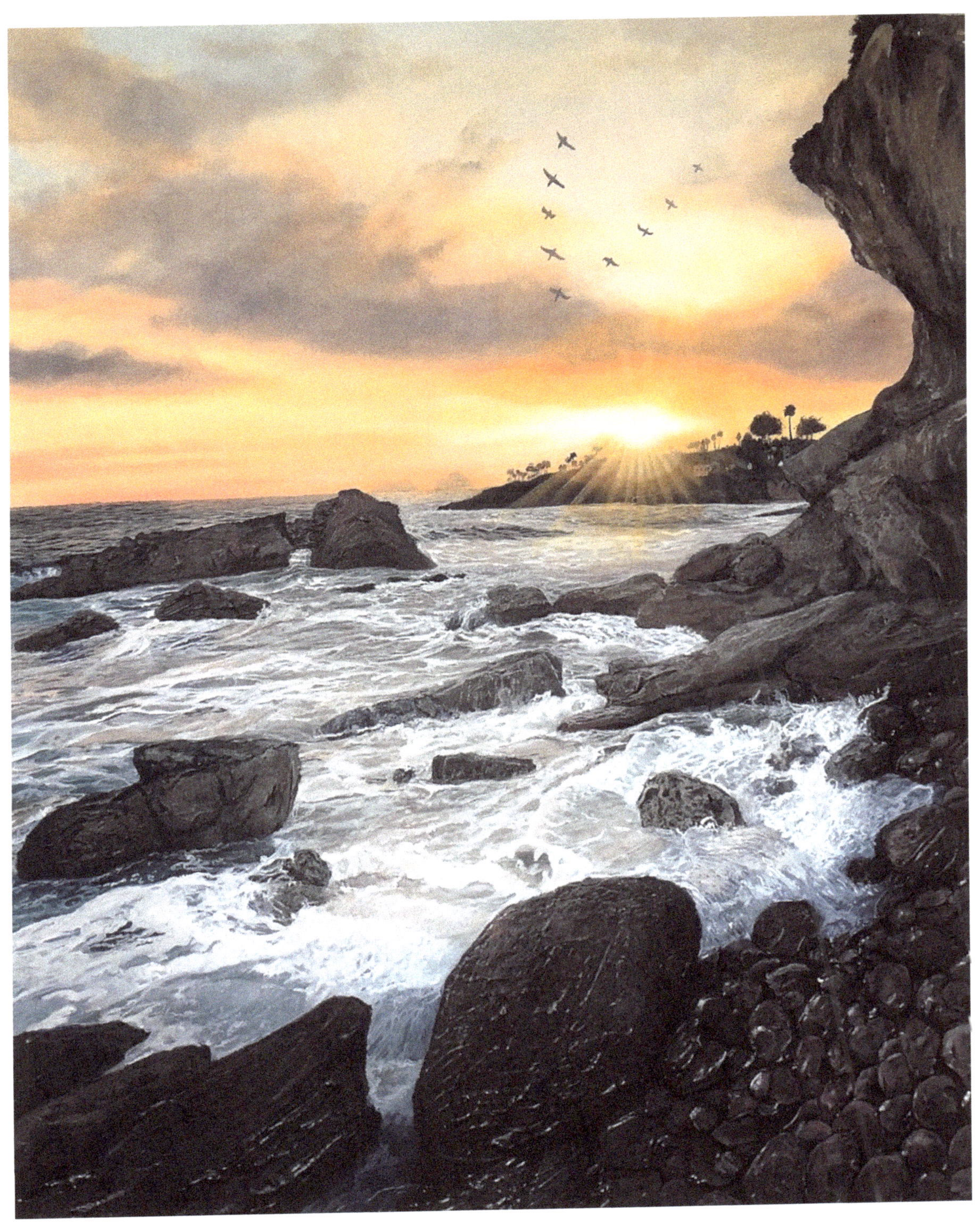

"Yesterday"

All images used are hand painted paintings and belong to the artist. The following references for these paintings, were used with permission from the following photographers:

A Promise pg 2 , Asaph Cueto
Not Too Long Ago pg. 4, Athena Grace
Time Is The Coin Of Your Life pg.8, Derek Madrigal
About This Time pg.10, Jack Hughes
Endurance pg.12, The Journey Of One Thousand Miles pg.14, Austin Perlmutter
A Reason To Hope pg.16, Scott Bakken
Sunsets And Storms pg.18, Austin Perlmutter
Wait And Hope pg.20, Hegyi Benjamin
Pure Heart pg.22, Jason Scottish
Forward pg.26, Anthony Berranger
Above All pg.28, It Is Time pg.30, Much More pg.32, If I Could pg.34, Austin Perlmutter
Deep Calls To Deep pg.36, Jared Kreiss
Set Apart pg.38, Empathy pg.40, Austin Perlmutter
Gratitude pg.42, George Bozouris
Knowledge pg.44, Austin Perlmutter
Humility pg.46, Jason Fenmore
Shalom pg.48, Sarah Afiqah Rodgers
But The Greatest Is pg.50, Jerret Lau
Courage pg.52, Erick Ramirez
Perseverance pg.54, Rod Trevino
Well Done pg.56, Chris Henry
Do Not Worry pg. 58, Austin Permutter
Receptivity pg.60, Erick Ramirez
Yesterday pg.62, Kevin Blim

Special Thanks

I would also like to acknowledge the help and support of Ioana. I don't know how or if I would've come this far without you. Your humility and love have humbled and exalted me.

Thank you to my editor, Katie. Your gift, kindness, and understanding of this were so needed. Thank you for all of your hard work.

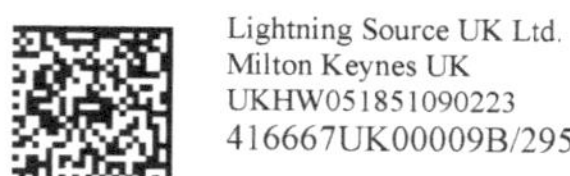

Lightning Source UK Ltd.
Milton Keynes UK
UKHW051851090223
416667UK00009B/295

9 781664 239098